HOW TO
POO
ON HOLIDAY

First published in 2011 by Prion
An imprint of the Carlton Publishing Group
20 Mortimer Street
London W1T 3JW

10 9 8 7 6 5 4 3

Editorial Manager: Roland Hall
Design: Stephen Cary, Emily Clarke, Sailesh Patel, James Pople
Production: Dawn Cameron
Photograph on page 11 © iStockphoto.com

ISBN 978-1-85375-811-9

Printed in Italy

HOW TO
POO
ON HOLIDAY

This practical guide to foreign toilet
hardware and customs will ease your
passage when travelling abroad

Mats & Enzo

PRION

CONTENTS

INTRODUCTION

Every year when the holidays are approaching it's the same thing. We all begin to fret. Holidays are great, but the idea of abandoning the comfy toilets of our homes for all those holiday toilets that are always broken, smell bad or are a challenge to use is always a source of stress. It's unavoidable, because the toilets at holiday destinations tend to be full of surprises. And we need not go to the other end of the world to find toilet trouble: how many campsites still boast those odd squat toilets that make the campers return to a very primitive position when relieving themselves? Worse yet, toilets at holiday destinations tend to have the thinnest of walls and enormous gaps between the door and the floor, making it easy for passers-by to observe the proceedings inside.

Yes, it is quite understandable that in such conditions some just can't manage to do their deed.

And then there are other dangers: how does one not suffocate whilst in a hermetically closed plastic mobile toilet that has been in the hot sun all day, with temperatures reaching over 55°C? And what to do when we get stuck in a dilapidated toilet because the lock hasn't been oiled in the last 15 years? As for the more exotic countries, you might just as well never venture there with all the dangers lurking in those loos.

Human nature can be a source of endless wonder, with the imagination in the habits and techniques relating to toilets that different cultures have shaped over centuries. A good example that you have surely heard about are the Japanese toilets. Their elaborate design can lead to many dangers for those not familiar with them (a water jet mistakenly set at 95 degrees... it burns). Travellers on longer visits to more remote countries must also have a certain openness of spirit to endure the toilet habits there. We will show you some

6

of them in this book, but would warmly recommend you to stay away from such countries if the simple fact that someone is looking at you while you're doing your deed can block the passage for you. In certain areas of Papua-New Guinea, for example, the whole village will gather to look at you, and when you're finished, they will perform a little celebratory dance.

With the increase in travel in recent years, we needed a serious book on the subject of holiday toilets, toilet customs and traditions of far-away people, and ways to manage toilet related issues in order to avoid Holiday Poo Syndrome (inability to relieve yourself when on holiday).

Don't get to this state; all the solutions can be found in this book.

The Holiday Poo Syndrome and its stages

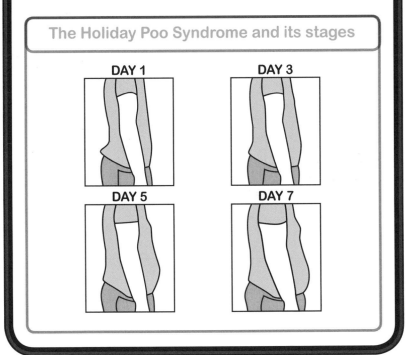

DAY 1

DAY 3

DAY 5

DAY 7

And this book is now before you

In it we have endeavoured to deal with all the problems that one can encounter on holiday, should they take place in the UK, in Europe or in exotic countries. We visited countless holiday destinations in order to understand the difficulties that foreigners can encounter during their travels. While everyone was enjoying their holidays, we were hard at work. We went, laptop in hand, to all sorts of installations and asked the locals to give us demonstrations in order to understand how such often-rudimentary facilities should be used and what the appropriate customs were. We also talked with holiday makers suffering poo-related trouble at French and Spanish camping grounds or holiday resorts, in order to help them and ease their Holiday Poo Syndrome.

It is on the basis of such diligent and detailed work – that nobody has done before – that we elaborated all the techniques suggested in this book.

Read this book before going on holiday and, if possible, train at home to prepare for situations that you could encounter at your holiday destination (turn on the heat to simulate summer time if necessary). We are convinced that if you master the techniques we will show you in this book, you will end up enjoying going to the toilet during your holidays. Yes, it is possible. There are, for example, toilets high in the mountains with views that will take your breath away, or toilets with transparent floors on boats that let you enjoy a view of the underwater world while you're doing your deed, or toilets with magical decorations in Cambodia... All inspirations for great photos to bring back from your holiday!

Toilets are also small spaces that facilitate new encounters, as long as you keep them casual: start a conversation only with someone washing their hands and who has obviously finished – somebody entering the toilets will never be very open to conversation.

You will be encouraged to know that many readers of this book have gone on to start blogs on world toilets, when before, they could not even leave their homes from fear of the dangers of more rudimentary toilets. Incredible progress!

This book will be your welcome travel companion in the years to come, and our biggest reward will be to receive a photo of you, smiling and relaxed in an exotic toilet that would not be welcoming to most people.

THE HOLIDAY TOILET EXPERT

Steven Gooper is a world renowned expert on all issues related to toilet attendance when on holiday. A true globe-trotter, he learned how to say "Where is the toilet?" and "How do you use this strange toilet brush?" in 240 world languages, as well as in dialects of tribes living in remote regions. He is also campaigning with tour guides around the world to make sure that travellers aren't left without information on the different types of local toilet installations, as well as to finally make it mandatory that an introduction to local toilet habits be always included as part of tour programmes.

Steven Gooper is advocating a completely new philosophy: going to the toilet in a foreign country is not a problem but a true source of pleasure. His learned advice will help you, too, to enjoy doing your deed on holiday.

Steven Gooper is passionate about toilets outside of his research as well. He has invented inflatable toilets. While still relatively unknown outside professional circles, they are sure to flood the market once widely available – unfortunately some accidents and falls during first homologation tests have caused some delays in their commercialisation. Steven has also collected over 200 toilet brushes from all corners of the world. His favourite is a gnu-hair brush with an ivory handle that a chief of an African village gave him in exchange for a demonstration of western practices.

We are immensely honoured that Steven Gooper has agreed to provide the expertise and vision for this book. His advice has changed our lives, and it is about to change yours. We will thank him in advance in your name.

MAKE THE HOLIDAY TOILET YOUR OWN

You have rented a villa or a small apartment for your holidays. The first thing you need to examine when you walk in is the toilet. All too often we wait until we feel the urge to test the new toilet for the first time, thus finding out a major problem only when it's already too late. Don't ruin your holidays: get into the routine of always performing the TSCL (Toilet Safety Check List). It will take you no more than 5 minutes.

1

Check first of all that toilet paper is available, and that not just one quarter of a roll remains. Make sure also that there is ample stock of toilet paper within arm's reach – this will prevent you or a member of your family from having to stomp around the premises penguin-style, pants around the ankles, asking if anyone has brought emergency toilet paper or has an old newspaper to spare.

2

Make sure that there is a toilet brush. This will prevent you or a member of your family from having to flush 6 or 7 times to try to eliminate the skid marks you left when doing your deed. Check also that it is a quality toilet brush. The owners of holiday rentals often try to save money by buying brushes made in China that cost no more than a few pence, but often end up bending or worse, breaking while being used.

3

Check if the flush works by testing it on an empty toilet. If the water doesn't come at first, try opening the valve. This simple test eliminates the danger of having to spend the first day of your holiday manually flushing toilets with the help of pots and pans full of water.

4

Make sure that there isn't any strange art hung on the walls of the toilet. It will most likely disturb you while attempting to do your deed. For example, a reproduction of the Mona Lisa will make you feel like she's watching you with her knowing smile during your efforts. Same goes for large portraits of the owner of the rental. It will block you. Turn those paintings around immediately.

5

Make sure that there is a toilet deodorizer in the toilet, that it is not empty, that the perfume is pleasing to you and that it is not too strong. There's nothing worse than an empty can of toilet deodorizer after you have stunk up the toilet of your rental villa. Also, coming out of the toilet smelling of the cheapest of air fresheners (i.e. lavender mixed with pine nuts) will not do you any favours. Invest in a new, quality deodorizer. The success of your holiday depends on it.

6

Make sure that there are magazines corresponding to the tastes of each occupant of your holiday abode. If none are provided, buy them at the nearest newspaper stand. The preferred toilet reading for the ladies will be some gossip rags, the men will enjoy some car magazines, while the children will want some comics. Never opt for broadsheet newspapers; they are especially hard to handle when one is doing one's deed, impossible to fold back, and have the annoying tendency to absorb water.

TEST: "ARE YOU A TOILET FREAK?"

Would you like to know your attitude towards toilets on holiday? Will your enjoyment of holidays depend on the toilets? Take this test and find out of the idea of being far away from your own toilet is a source of stress for you!

1. You take with you a trailer full of toilet paper to make sure you will have enough for the entire holiday. You never know what one can find in a foreign land.
2. You call the local tourist office several times and ask them to explain the functioning of the local toilets, and to provide you with an updated map of public toilets in the region.
3. You replicate the local climate and conditions at home to exercise: heating to the max, solar protection cream on your buttocks, doing your deed in the garden at night and in the rain.
4. You find an insurance company that includes "I can't do it" in the list of possible reasons for repatriation.
5. You download an iPhone application that chases away the poop flies.
6. You memorize this book and make your wife and children quiz you every day.
7. You take with you 6 different types of anti-diarrhea medicine as well as 9 different laxatives.
8. You find out how to do a "no residue" diet during your holiday.
9. You ask questions in travel forums and Yahoo Questions & Answers to get first-hand information about the toilet situation of your destination.
10. You see a therapist to help you prepare psychologically before departure.
11. The first thing you do after arriving is to look for toilets.
12. During your holiday you make sure that a toilet is always available in the radius of 30m, and if it is occupied, you start panicking because you might have to go.
13. You refuse to go on a day trip if you haven't been able to do your deed beforehand.

14. You have already decided to abort your family vacation and return home because the toilet is not to your liking.
15. You have already thought of never going on holiday again in order to avoid the stress of having to face unfamiliar toilet arrangements.

You have answered 'No' to all of the questions above

Bravo, but why did you then buy this book? Your money would have been better spent on a book on knitting, the well-being of sheep, or the influence of the moon's changes on gardening.

You have answered 'Yes' to at least one of the questions above

You have a problem with toilets on holiday. A study suggests that such issues stem from trauma in your early childhood. Did your mother lock you in the toilet on holiday when you weren't behaving? Were you punished for breaking a collectable toilet brush? Were you forced to wipe off with magazine pages because your parents forgot to bring toilet paper? Relax, you have nothing to worry about: this book will help you face your issues and let you move forward in your life.

You answered 'Yes' to all of the questions above

You have a grave problem! You have several options. 1. Take your vacations in maximum 10 km radius from your home. That way you can return to your own toilet in case of an emergency. 2. Find a support group with people who have similar problems, entitled "I, too, can do my deed in toilets other than mine." 3. Fast during your holidays.

USEFUL "HOW TO POO" FOREIGN LANGUAGE PHRASEBOOK

If you are embarking on a holiday, take with you this phrasebook as it will certainly come in useful. Keep it in hand and you will avoid many problems.

(**ENGLISH** – FRENCH – SPANISH – ITALIAN)

Where is the toilet?
FRA Où sont les toilettes ? FRA
ESP ¿Dónde están los baños? ESP
ITA Dove sono i servizi igienici? ITA

Could you lend me some toilet paper?
FRA Pourriez-vous me prêter du papier ? FRA
ESP ¿Podría prestarme el papel? ESP
ITA Mi presti la carta igienica? ITA

I am sorry, I broke the toilet brush.
FRA Je suis désolé, j'ai cassé la balayette. FRA
ESP Lo siento, me rompió la escoba. ESP
ITA Mi dispiace, ho rotto la scopa. ITA

I apologize, I stunk it up.
FRA Je suis désolé, j'ai tout pourri. FRA
ESP Lo siento, tengo todo podrido. ESP
ITA Mi dispiace, ho tutto marcito. ITA

Did you eat cabbage yesterday?
FRA Vous avez mangé du chou hier ? FRA
ESP Se comió la col ayer? ESP
ITA Lei ieri ha mangiato cavolo? ITA

Which toilet paper would you recommend?
(FRA) Quel papier toilette me conseillez vous? (FRA)
(ESP) ¿Qué papel higiénico me recomiendan? (ESP)
(ITA) Quale carta igienica mi consiglia? (ITA)

What is the most reputable brand of toilet paper in your country?
(FRA) Quelle est la marque de papier toilette la plus réputée dans votre pays? (FRA)
(ESP) ¿Qué marca de papel higiénico el más famoso en su país? (ESP)
(ITA) Che marca di carta igienica il più famoso nel suo paese? (ITA)

Is this toilet paper three-layered?
(FRA) Ce papier toilette est il bien triple couche? (FRA)
(ESP) Este papel higiénico, aunque es de triple capa? (ESP)
(ITA) Questa carta igienica anche se è triplo strato? (ITA)

Don't the toilets have doors in your country?
(FRA) Il n'y a pas de porte dans les toilettes de votre pays? (FRA)
(ESP) No hay puerta en el baño de su país? (ESP)
(ITA) Non c'è nessuna porta nel bagno del vostro paese? (ITA)

I am sorry, I farted.
(FRA) Désolé, j'ai pété. (FRA)
(ESP) Lo siento, me tiró un pedo. (ESP)
(ITA) Mi dispiace, ho scoreggiato. (ITA)

I have a cigar in my mouth.
(FRA) J'ai le cigare au bord des lèvres. (FRA)
(ESP) Tengo un cigarro en los labios. (ESP)
(ITA) Ho un sigaro sulle labbra. (ITA)

I am sorry, I confused the men's and women's toilets.
(FRA) Pardon, j'ai confondu toilettes homme et femme. (FRA)
(ESP) Lo siento, me confunde aseos masculinos y femeninos. (ESP)
(ITA) Scusa, ho confuso servizi igienici maschili e femminili. (ITA)

Are you ill?
(FRA) Vous êtes malade ? (FRA)
(ESP) Estás enfermo? (ESP)
(ITA) Stai male? (ITA)

Quick, leave, I have diarrhea.
(FRA) Sortez vite, j'ai la diarrhée (FRA)
(ESP) Salir rápido, tengo diarrea (ESP)
(ITA) Uscire velocemente, ho diarrea (ITA)

It's coming out.
(FRA) Ca pousse. (FRA)
(ESP) Crece. (ESP)
(ITA) Cresce (ITA)

Do you have Immodium?
(FRA) Avez-vous de l'Imodium? (FRA)
(ESP) ¿Tiene el Imodium? (ESP)
(ITA) Avete la Imodium? (ITA)

Be careful, the toilet is overflowing.
(FRA) Attention, la cuvette déborde. (FRA)
(ESP) Tenga en cuenta que la copa rebosa. (ESP)
(ITA) Si prega di notare che la coppa trabocca. (ITA)

How exactly does this toilet work?
(FRA) Comment fonctionnent ces toilettes exactement? (FRA)
(ESP) ¿Cómo funciona exactamente estos servicios? (ESP)
(ITA) Come esattamente queste toilette? (ITA)

I'm so annoyed, my phone fell into the toilet.
(FRA) Je suis embêté, mon téléphone est tombé dans les toilettes. (FRA)
(ESP) Estoy cabreado, mi teléfono cayó en el inodoro. (ESP)
(ITA) Sono incazzato, il mio telefono è caduto nel gabinetto. (ITA)

Stop knocking, it's occupied!
(FRA) Arrêtez de frapper à la porte, c'est occupé! (FRA)
(ESP) Deje de llamar a la puerta, que está ocupado! (ESP)
(ITA) Stop a bussare alla porta, è occupato! (ITA)

Why are there five buttons on this toilet?
(FRA) Pourquoi y a-t-il cinq boutons sur ces toilettes? (FRA)
(ESP) ¿Por qué hubo cinco botones en el inodoro? (ESP)
(ITA) Perché era lì cinque pulsanti sul water? (ITA)

You forgot to close your zip.
(FRA) Vous avez oublié de fermer votre braguette. (FRA)
(ESP) Usted se olvidó de cerrar su marcha. (ESP)
(ITA) Hai dimenticato di chiudere il tuo volo. (ITA)

Is it you who stunk it up like that?
(FRA) C'est vous qui avez tout pourri? (FRA)
(ESP) Son ustedes los que están podridos? (ESP)
(ITA) Siete voi che siete marci? (ITA)

Do you have the 'Spruce tree with lavender' toilet deodorizer?
(FRA) Vous reste-t-il une bombe de désodorisant 'Sapin vert à la lavande'? (FRA)
(ESP) Que tienes ahí un desodorante en aerosol, abeto verde lavanda? (ESP)
(ITA) Hai c'è un deodorante spray, verde abete Lavanda '? (ITA)

Please don't skip the queue for the toilet!
(FRA) S'il vous plait, on ne double pas dans le la queue des toilettes! (FRA)
(ESP) Por favor, no se duplica en la cola del baño! (ESP)
(ITA) Per favore, non matrimoniale in coda alla toilette! (ITA)

Don't touch me!
FRA Ne me touchez pas ! FRA
ESP No me toques! ESP
ITA Non mi toccare! ITA

1€ to shit, that's outrageous!
FRA 1€ pour chier, c'est vraiment abusé! FRA
ESP 1€ a mierda, lo que realmente abusados! ESP
ITA €1 a merda, davvero abusato! ITA

Your toilet paper itches, my skin is irritated.
FRA Votre papier toilette gratte, j'ai des irritations. FRA
ESP Su inodoro rascador artículo, irritaciones. ESP
ITA La carta igienica raschietto, ho irritazioni. ITA

Is there a discount if I take 100 rolls?
FRA Faites vous une remise si je prends 100 rouleaux? FRA
ESP Hacer un descuento si tomo 100 rollos? ESP
ITA Ti fanno uno sconto se prendo 100 rotoli? ITA

I'm stuck in the toilet, help me!
FRA Je suis bloqué dans les toilettes, aidez moi. FRA
ESP Estoy atascado en el baño, que me ayude. ESP
ITA Sono bloccato in bagno, mi aiuti. ITA

Can somebody bring me a roll?
FRA Quelqu'un peut il m'apporter un rouleau? FRA
ESP ¿Puede alguien darme un rollo? ESP
ITA Qualcuno può darmi un rotolo? ITA

How much is this toilet seat?
(FRA) Combien coûte cette lunette de WC? (FRA)
(ESP) ¿Cuánto cuesta este asiento del inodoro? (ESP)
(ITA) Quanto costa questa sedile del water? (ITA)

Is the sheet usable on both sides?
(FRA) La feuille est elle recto-verso ? (FRA)
(ESP) La hoja es de doble cara? (ESP)
(ITA) Il foglio è a doppia faccia? (ITA)

Can you lend me your gossip magazine?
(FRA) Pouvez-vous me prêter votre magazine people? (FRA)
(ESP) ¿Me puede prestar su revista de celebridades? (ESP)
(ITA) Potrebbe prestarmi la tua rivista celebrità? (ITA)

I have to leave you; I'm going to recycle my delicious lunch.
(FRA) Je vous laisse, je vais recycler le délicieux repas de ce midi. (FRA)
(ESP) Os dejo, voy a reciclar de una deliciosa comida al mediodía. (ESP)
(ITA) Vi lascio, voglio riciclare un delizioso pasto a mezzogiorno. (ITA)

I already feel lighter.
(FRA) Je me sens déjà plus léger. (FRA)
(ESP) Ya me siento más ligero. (ESP)
(ITA) Mi sento già più leggero. (ITA)

Won't you close the door?
(FRA) Vous ne fermez pas la porte? (FRA)
(ESP) No cierre la puerta? (ESP)
(ITA) Non chiudere la porta? (ITA)

Get out, you've been in the toilet for an hour!
(FRA) Sortez, ça fait une heure que vous êtes dans les toilettes! (FRA)
(ESP) ¡Fuera, ha sido una vez que estás en el baño! (ESP)
(ITA) Fuori, è stata una volta che sei in bagno! (ITA)

USEFUL "HOW TO POO" FOREIGN LANGUAGE PHRASEBOOK

OK, is it my turn now?
(FRA) Bon, c'est mon tour? (FRA)
(ESP) Bueno, es mi turno? (ESP)
(ITA) Beh, è il mio turno? (ITA)

Did you do this?
(FRA) C'est vous qui avez fait ça? (FRA)
(ESP) Fuiste tú quien lo hizo? (ESP)
(ITA) Vi era chi è stato? (ITA)

Do you have souvenir toilet brushes?
(FRA) Avez-vous des balayettes souvenirs? (FRA)
(ESP) ¿Tiene cepillos recuerdos? (ESP)
(ITA) Avete pennelli ricordi? (ITA)

PROBLEMS YOU CAN ENCOUNTER IN FAR AWAY, EXOTIC LANDS

The toilets can be full of surprises when you are far from home. What can you do if you encounter an unfamiliar toilet setup? What to do when a lion attacks you while you're doing your deed? How do you not freeze your bum off when taking a dump on an iceberg?

On the following pages you will find solutions to all problems that you may encounter when you feel the urge in far away countries.

The Golden Rules

1. Always carry a safety toilet paper roll in your bag (many countries don't provide it, or provide painful alternatives).
2. Avoid local specialties (you will pay dearly each time after you break this rule).
3. Never pay a stranger who offers to teach you local toilet use (9 times out of 10 it's a scam).
4. When doing your deed outdoors, choose a higher ground as it allows you to see potential dangers approaching (wild animals, a park ranger, a bus full of tourists...)
5. The first words you should learn in a foreign language aren't "hello" and "thank you", but rather "gents", "ladies", "toilet paper" and "toilet brush".

The situation:

You are relieving yourself behind a tree when a lion appears and starts approaching you dangerously. He does not seem to understand what you are doing and growls menacingly.

SOLUTION: Beating the Drum

1. Swiftly take off your belt and arm yourself with a stick (a BIG stick).
2. Stand up, puff up your chest and beat it with your fists in order to make it clear to him that you are the dominant species – never mind that your pants are round your ankles.
3. Indicate to the lion with the help of your stick that he should in fact jump to the other side of the grove.
4. If he doesn't obey, smack your belt like a circus animal trainer would.
5. Once the lion is on the other side of the grove, make giant leaps towards your Jeep (don't waste time pulling up your trousers).

Expert Opinion

Don't try the 'Irritated Skunk' technique in this situation – which of course is the technique of projecting a nauseating odour in the enemy's face. It does not work with lions.

Testimonial

I must be emanating a particular odour because not a minute had passed when a giraffe, two gnus, an elephant and three rhinos came to see what animal could produce such a smell.
Giles, 28, assistant, Swindon

YOU DON'T KNOW HOW TO SAY "TOILET" IN THE LOCAL LANGUAGE

The situation:

You are walking around a foreign town when suddenly the urge overtakes you. But there is a problem: you don't know how to ask where the toilets are in the local language.

SOLUTION: The One-Man Show

1. Don't worry; the Universal Language can be used in this situation.
2. Stop the first stranger in the street who comes your way.
3. Show him what the issue is by holding your stomach and grimacing, as if in pain.
4. Hold your nose on top of that.
5. If he doesn't understand, squat and make loud farting noises with your mouth.
6. Once he understands and points you to the nearest toilet, you should probably signal that while it was very kind of him to have helped you, he probably shouldn't accompany you.

Expert Opinion

Be careful: several tribes in Papua-New Guinea consider making fart noises on another tribe's territory to be a declaration of war.

Testimonial

He understood nothing... In the end I had to open a chocolate bar and place it close to my butt so that he finally understood what I was trying to do. I offered him the chocolate bar to thank him, but he didn't want it...
Kenneth, 33, VP of marketing, Abingdon

YOU ARE INSIDE A PYRAMID IN EGYPT

The situation:

You are on a tour of an Egyptian pyramid when a sudden urge to go overcomes you. But there is a problem: you are deep under the pyramid and it would take you well over an hour to get out and reach the nearest toilet.

1. Ask the tour guide quietly if perchance the Egyptians placed any toilets in the pyramids. (His answer will probably be "No, no shit here! Impossible!"
2. Distance yourself from the group and discreetly do your deed in a hidden corner.
3. While doing it, please be careful not to soil the hieroglyphs on the walls; each coloured line is of capital importance in their deciphering.
4. Cover your deed with a bit of sand.
5. Use the papyrus you bought in the gift shop as toilet paper (don't feel bad; they are made by the kilometre in China).

Expert Opinion

According to my research, the Egyptians also did their deed in profile.

Testimonial

Obviously I was not the first to encounter this problem inside a pyramid because dozens of merchants were following our group and offered me buckets and papyrus-like toilet paper, yelling: "You, shit? You, SHIT?"
Owen, 32, producer, Leeds

IN A WILDERNESS PARK; A RANGER WALKS IN ON YOU

The situation:

You distance yourself from the group to relieve yourself unnoticed. But there is a problem: a ranger stepped into your deed and is coming towards the group, looking angry.

SOLUTION: The Chuck Norris

1. Gather your face into a shocked and outraged expression while listening to the ranger explain that someone did their deed in the little botanical garden where all the endangered species of the park are grown.
2. Listen to the ranger explain how and why we should respect the endemic species (you might learn something).
3. When he has finished, turn to face the group.
4. Tell them: "The ranger is right; I find this outrageous as well!"
5. Finish by saying: "How the person who did this will be able to look at himself in the mirror, I don't know. Gerry, I wish you luck."

Expert Opinion

If you prefer fibrous organic food, contact the park administration. The rangers often welcome donations of organic compost and sometimes even remunerate it. Keep in mind, however, that they will ask you for the last three receipts from your organic food store and will study them carefully.

Testimonial

The ranger was a national specialist in tracking wild animals. He sniffed my deed for a few seconds and immediately turned towards me. The result: a $1,500 fine for "Doing the deed in a protected zone category A++."
Alan, 42, production controller, Edinburgh

YOU ARE AT THE NORTH POLE

The situation:

You are far in the North, with the whitest eternal snow everywhere. But there is a problem: the temperature is at -40°C. If you uncover your buttocks, they could freeze instantly.

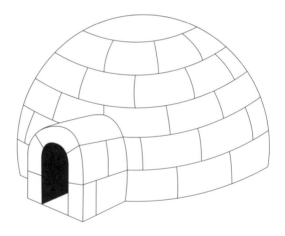

SOLUTION: The Soviet Method

1. Don't panic. An old and proven Soviet method exists for just such situations.
2. Bring out your gas stove.
3. Set it to 1 (the minimum) and place it on the snow.
4. Take off your pants and squat just enough to be able to hover above the gas stove.
5. Do your deed (attention: don't dump it on the flame, but just next to it).
6. Get dressed quickly, because in a matter of minutes, dozens of seals and reindeer will start gathering around you, attracted by the minerals that you have just let out.

Expert Opinion

Don't forget to hide your deed (which will be deeply frozen in less than a minute) under a bit of snow. It would not be appropriate to disturb the pristine whiteness of the North.

Testimonial

I wasn't balanced and got my buttocks too close to the stove. It started to smell of grilled pork... and I got second degree burns. I was mortified and so embarrassed an hour later at the hospital!
Laura, 28, telecoms specialist, Birmingham

COMMUNAL TOILETS WITH NO WALLS

The situation:

Tired of overly touristy destinations you decide to visit a country that has not been affected by mass tourism. It was adventure that you wanted, and you find it: when you arrive you realize that the toilets are communal and have no walls. You will have to do your deed amongst dozens of locals who are doing it too.

SOLUTION: Team Effort

1. Come armed with a good magazine.
2. Enter into the wide space with over 30 toilets one next to the other, with courtesy separations of just 50 cm.
3. With a big smile, say hello to all other occupants who are in the throes of passage.
4. Take a seat, and don't laugh nervously each time a neighbour passes gas.
5. To avoid blockage due to stress stemming from such an unusual installation, focus completely on a story in your magazine.
6. Do your deed.
7. Ask the person holding the only toilet paper roll to please pass it to you.
8. Say goodbye.

Expert Opinion

I have already seen these kinds of toilets in an enormous factory in China. The toilets were in a hangar the size of a football field, with 30 rows of 20 toilets each. It made me think of battery chicken farm. Two giant ventilators continuously dispersed 6 litres of toilet deodorizer 'Fleur de Lotus' per minute.

Testimonial

When I went to Gladezistan, they had communal toilets. When I finished my deed, an old lady came and brought me some toilet paper. She stayed in front of me and waited for me to finish, so she could take the paper. I had to tell her "Thank you, but I can manage by myself." and "I can't do it if you keep staring at me!" Annoying...
Tim, 25, senior account manager, Telford

YOU FALL IN THE SEPTIC TANK

You are in a foreign land. You enter a bamboo toilet stall. The seat doesn't seem very stable. You get your confirmation moments later when you sit down: it cracks under your weight and you fall into the septic tank.

SOLUTION: The Brown Butterfly Technique

1. As you feel yourself falling, spread your arms in order to break the fall and avoid getting your head under… ahem, water.
2. Hold your breath; the methane surrounding you could suffocate you.
3. Don't call out for help; this is a situation you should keep to yourself.
4. Make wide movements with your legs in order to push yourself up and grab what is left of your seat.
5. Pull yourself up and come out of the tank.
6. Run towards the nearest river or beach and throw yourself in the water.
7. Never tell this story to your friends. NEVER.

Expert Opinion

An American study has found that such things occur to over 1,000 people globally each year. The victims need on average three to four years to recover from the trauma of such a misadventure.

Testimonial

This happened to me here in England. I fell into the tank of a plastic toilet that was full of a fluorescent blue liquid. I managed to get out, but my skin was blue for two years. I never told anyone what had happened to me. My family was very worried; they thought I was slowly metamorphosing into a Smurf.

Tony, 34, R&D, Leighton Buzzard

YOU HAD A VERY SPICY DINNER
THE NIGHT BEFORE

The situation:

During a holiday in a foreign country you thought it would be nice to taste a typical local dish. The fact that it was so spicy that even locals avoided it didn't scare you. It was a painful experience, and you fear what is to follow the next day.

SOLUTION: The Milky Way

1. As soon as you start feeling the urge to go the next morning, grab a carton of cold milk.
2. Go to the toilet, armed with your milk carton.
3. Proceed with your deed. When you start feeling the burn, pour a generous amount of milk on the affected area.
4. Repeat the milk rinse as often as needed (however, manage the quantities so that you don't run out of milk too soon).
5. Don't come out of the toilet with an empty milk carton; people could quickly ascertain what your problem is.

Expert Opinion

If milk isn't available, take the toilet brush, put its handle in your mouth and bite it hard.

Testimonial

I tried to cool the area off with the only thing I had available: an air freshener called "Polar Fresh". It contains alcohol, and it ended up burning twice as much!
Jay, 42, salesman, Bath

YOU ARE IN JAPAN, FACED WITH AN 'OLD-FASHIONED' TOILET

The situation:

During a trip to Japan you decide to go and explore secret Japan and its most remote villages. When the need emerges, you are faced with a traditional Japanese toilet dating back from the beginning of the last century.

SOLUTION: The Kawasaki

1. Careful, these toilets have a meaning. Respect them.
2. Position yourself as if you were mounting a motorbike (the thicker part of the toilet should be in front).
3. Bend your knees to lower yourself near the pot.
4. Do your deed.
5. Wipe off (careful, due to balance problems, tourists often find themselves falling backwards).
6. Flush.

Expert Opinion

Some tourists believe that this toilet is a urinal in the ground. Such tourists then stand above this 'urinal' and get into the push-up position to pee.

Testimonial

I asked a local lady to explain to me how this toilet works, but she spoke no English. She therefore called a friend, who called another friend, who called another friend... After 10 minutes there were 18 of them around the toilet. They were all frantically gesticulating and explaining in Japanese how I should poo properly.
Dick, 37, broker, Colchester

The situation:

A few hours after arriving to Japan a strong urge comes over you. For the first time in your life you will have to use their state-of-the-art toilets. (We have previously presented the solution to this problem in our earlier oeuvre, *How to Poo at Work*.)

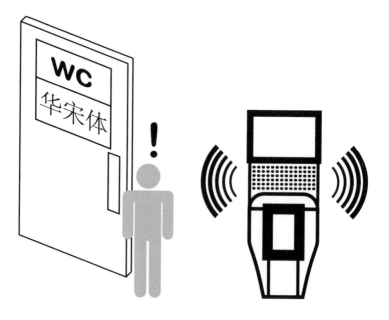

SOLUTION: Extreme Prudence

1. Do not ask anyone for help; in the Japanese culture, asking for help when going to the toilet is considered an insult. You have to figure it out on your own!
2. Approach the seat, remove the necessary pieces of clothing, but do not touch the seat. It may have sensors linked with the flushing mechanism.
3. Sit down, do what you came in to do as gently as possible, and get dressed.
4. Once finished, do not flush: open the door of your stall first.
5. Close your eyes, cover up your face with your hands, and quickly press on all the buttons simultaneously.
6. Run as fast as possible to leave the toilet and find a safe zone.
7. On the way, never turn back no matter what happens, and never stop, whatever may be going on behind you.
8. Take your hands from your face only when you have reached your safe zone.

Expert Opinion

When facing a new system, prudence is always a good policy. Personally, I learned Japanese before coming to Japan only to be able to read the instructions for their toilets. They can be up to 250 pages and come with hundreds of diagrams!

Testimonial

When I realized that I would have to do it for the first time in a toilet with a new high-tech system, I thought to myself that this could be a new and interesting experience. Perfume spraying out, water rinse… What's not to like, I thought – until I saw the tweezers coming out. I ran as fast as I could; I think I got out in the nick of time!
George, 43, Assistant Director, Stockton

YOU ARE IN A FOREIGN COUNTRY, FACED WITH A SQUAT TOILET

The situation:

You are in a foreign land where they only have squat toilets — known also in some countries as the Turkish toilets. These perilous toilets require some knowledge for safe use.

SOLUTION: Step by Step

1. Whatever the circumstances, never go in there in flip flops; way too risky!
2. Careful, you should know that there is the right direction to use them: you should place your feet on the two steps on each side of the hole, with your bum over the hole, facing the door.
3. Lower your trousers, but not too low as it may touch the toilet.
4. Carefully do your deed, always keeping in mind that you may get soiled by the dropping… objects.
5. Open the door, flush and run. The flush is almost always aimed badly and may cause polluted overflowing or flooding.

Expert Opinion

Such toilets are very healthy. The position they impose puts the colon in a very natural position which provides for a 1.7 times faster and much more thorough emptying of the bowels. The squatting also provides a good exercise for your legs.

Testimonial

In India they also have squat toilets, which come equipped with two jugs of water for cleaning. It was very hot when I was there and I thought that the water was there for hydration, so I stupidly drank from it. I had diarrhoea for two months.
Alex, 46, banker, Tokyo

YOU ARE ATTACKED BY AN ELEPHANT

The situation:

You are in an elephant park in Asia. As you sit down in a slightly dodgy and unstable toilet fashioned out of bamboo sticks, an elephant that obviously followed the smell sticks his trunk through the gap under the door and tries to grab your leg.

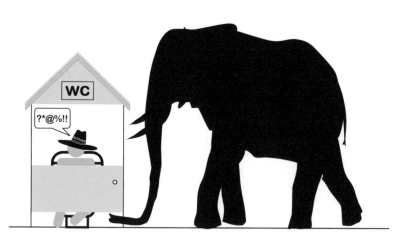

SOLUTION: The Ninja-Dumbo

1. Hold in the flatulence; you risk attracting another elephant, which could complicate your situation.
2. Grab the toilet paper and stuff it in his trunk. Your objective: suffocate the elephant.
3. If the elephant doesn't get the message, arm yourself with a toilet brush and bang on his trunk with it.
4. If he still doesn't get it, empty the air freshener into his nostrils. This should make him leave.
5. Take a photo of the elephant when you come out of the toilet in order to be able to brag to your friends at home that you made a dangerous wild animal run.

Expert Opinion

If someday we decided to make toilets for elephants, they would require toilet flushes of 640 litres and toilet paper with the diameter of a tractor tyre.

Testimonial

I was in complete panic, but fortunately it turned out it was only part of the games on offer in my resort. The elephant came to rinse my bum by splashing water from its trunk. Getting soaked with 30 litres of water up there – it's a bloody shock, believe me!
Andy, 32, auditor, Milton Keynes

YOU HAVE DIARRHOEA

You spend the holidays in an exotic country and get a bad case of diarrhoea. Don't be like all the dumb holiday-makers who try to continue their holidays without changing their plans. Accept your problem: spend the day in the toilet and try to make it fun with the help of our advice.

SOLUTION: The Cocooning Throne

1. Fill your coolbox as if you were going on a picnic in the mountains (plain rice must be on the menu).
2. Go to the toilet with the coolbox and get yourself settled. Cut a hole in your cushion and use it for more comfort.
3. Write your postcards while doing your deeds (your friends will never guess you wrote them in the toilet). Don't write things like: "I have the worst diarrhoea in history. I'm on my 18th roll of paper." Say only that you are having a great holiday and that the landscape is gorgeous (never mind that the landscape you are currently staring at is the toilet door; it won't make anyone jealous).
4. Don't forget the suncream. After nine hours under the toilet lamp that too will give you sunburn.
5. Bring three novels of at least 500 pages, rather than magazines.

Expert Opinion

Look at the bright side: a day of pushing will give you nice abs. You will be able to show them off at the beach, and they will also help you the next day when you'll be constipated due to all the rice you ate.

Testimonial

I had a great day. However, my family was furious. They had been knocking on the toilet door wanting to use the toilet, but I was listening to my iPod and didn't hear a thing.
Jimmy, Assistant, 44, London.

WORLD TOILETS - KEY PHRASES

TANZANIA

Mimi ni lazima kweli kupata ndani yake pamoja na pikipiki yako?
Do I really have to go in on a motorbike?

SOUTH AFRIKA

Dit is interessant wees om jou wild maar daar is werklik moet gaan.
**It's very interesting, all the wild animals you have here,
but I really have to go.**

SWITZERLAND

Vous pensez vraiment que je vais payer 7€ pour un rouleau?
**Do you really think that I will pay seven Euros
for a roll of toilet paper?**

INDONESIA

TIDAK, aku tidak membeli Anda foto souvenir Anda
NO, I will not buy your photo souvenir.

MOLDAVIA

Este inteligent sa gadila cu scaunul de toaleta din masina.
It's very clever how you made a toilet out of a car seat.

ITALY

pizza con le acciughe ho avuto uno strano effetto.
Your anchovy pizza has a strange effect.

ALBANIA

atë, ju paguani me peshë?
What, you have to pay by weight here?

GERMANY

Haben Sie wirklich brauchen diese Toiletten, die Sie sehen lassen,
was Sie getan haben?
Do you really need these toilets that let you
analyse and observe your deed?

AZERBAIJAN

Bəli, sonra donuz var, mənə bir dəqiqə buraxın.
Give me two minutes, yes, you will get it for your pigs after.

SAUDI ARABIA

أشعر بأن القرف الخاص بالإبل يراقبني آلآن
I have a feeling that your camel is observing me while I shit.

ARGENTINA

Puede por favor pregunte a los jugadores de acordeón
que me deje sola en el baño?
Could you please tell the accordion players to
leave me alone in the toilet?

AUSTRALIA

Next WC: 600 miles
No, I'm just not very hungry thanks

ARMENIA

Ձեր ընկերոչ կարող է դաղարեցնել նայում ինձ միչոցով
փոքրիկ պատուհանից
Could your friend please stop looking at me through the little window?

BAHAMAS

Pa sir, ki pa te yon pwason mawon! Mwen si li te yon chi.
No sir, that was not a brown fish! I am sure it was a shit.

GEORGIA

Ah? ეს არის შუა ეზოში წინ ყველას?
Ah? We do it in the courtyard, with everyone looking?

VIETNAM

cảm ơn bạn nhưng tôi thực sự không cần phải dựa vào
sự thành công kinh doanh
**Thank you, but I don't need you to push on my stomach
in order to succeed.**

BIELARUS

Не, кажу вам я не краў гэтую пэндзаль!
No, I'm telling you, I did not steal this toilet brush!

BRAZIL

o banheiro é o homem ou a mulher aqui?
Is this gents or ladies?

KENYA

Na msaada! rafiki yangu akaanguka katika shimo.
Help! My friend fell in the septic tank!

CAMBODIA

น้ำผึ้ง, ฉันบอกคุณจะต่อรองราคาของ 100 ม้วนสำหรับ 2€

**Darling, I'm telling you; 100 rolls of toilet paper
for 2 Euros is a great deal.**

CANADA

Hurry up!

Finish quickly Gerry, a moose is coming!

CHINA

你 了, 我没有下令250,000眼 状的金 。

**You must be mistaken; I haven't ordered 250,000 pairs of glasses
shaped as goldfish.**

COLOMBIA

no disparen, estoy tratando de mierda.

Don't shoot, I'm trying to shit.

CONGO

ndizi yako ni nzuri, lakini ni kweli wao wana laxative nguvu.

**Your bananas are good, that's true, but they have a
strong laxative effect.**

CUBA

no, mi cigarro no se caiga a la taza.

No, my cigar did not fall into the toilet.

DOMINICAN REPUBLIC

Yo se hará cargo de este cóctel!

I will never have this cocktail again!

WORLD TOILETS - KEY PHRASES

EGYPT

ⓜⓗ✠▬ⓜ ✠● ◐◆ •ⓜ ○ⓜ▢ⓜ ♎ⓜ ✠●

Incredible, one has to shit from profile as well...

SPAIN

Obviamente, las tapas no eran muy frescas.

Obviously the tapas weren't all that fresh.

UNITED STATES

Yes, we dump!

Yes, we poo!

FINLAND

Sinä lämpöä myös! se on vähintään 100 astetta puinen wc.

**Your heating is set way too high! It must be 100 degrees
in this wooden toilet!**

FRANCE

comment ça la dame pipi est en grève !?!

What do you mean the toilet lady is on strike?!

UGANDA

kweli kutoa kwa kula kuku wa?

You will really give this to the chickens to eat?

BURUNDI

Ambapo ni ya vyoo, mimi tu kuona nzi.
Where is the toilet? I can only see the flies.

INDIA

हे भगवान, यह जलता है.
Oh my God, it's burning.

AFGHANISTAN

.ما هفیظو نم ، منک رکشت مناوت یمن نم
Don't thank me, I'm only doing my duty.

JAPAN

それがこの事を動作しませんか、私はたわごとと思います。
How does this thing work? I just want to poo.

ROMANIA

Eu nu pot face dacă sunteţi în căutarea doamnă.
I can't do it if you are watching me, madam.

SWEDEN

är det ett träd för man eller kvinna?
Is this a men's or women's tree?

MALAYSIA

ini berus toilet?
Is this actually a toilet brush?

PHILIPPINES

Walang mga ito ay hindi ako na nakabasag ng bezel
No, I didn't break this toilet seat.

CAMPING ISSUES

Many vacationers choose to go camping for holidays. The fragile toilet installations and the proximity of other campers make campground a fertile area for new problems: people being able to observe your every move, toilets that are too far to reach in time, the gossip…

What should you do if your neighbour steals your toilet paper? What should you do if you are followed by a cloud of blue flies when you come out of the toilet?

Find out on following pages how you can go to the toilet without fear when camping, and have a great holiday.

The Golden Rules

1. Never go to the toilet with your neighbour (even if you really get along).
2. Don't stock your toilet paper outside of your tent (you risk someone will steal it or that the rain or dew will make it wet and render useless).
3. Avoid going during toilet rush hour (8.30am, 2pm, 7pm).
4. Always go to the toilet with only one mission (never come equipped for toilet multitasking, namely brushing teeth + washing dishes + the deed).
5. Pitch your tent close enough to, but also far enough from, the sanitaries (otherwise you will spend your holiday enveloped in nauseating smells and will have difficulty sleeping due to the noise of water and people farting during the night).

YOUR NEIGHBOUR AT THE CAMPGROUND STOLE YOUR STOCK OF TOILET PAPER

The situation:

You come back from the beach when you notice that your family pack of 64 rolls of toilet paper that was supposed to last you the whole vacation has disappeared. You are sure that it was your neighbour who stole it.

SOLUTION: The Egyptian Vengeance

1. Do not file a complaint, neither at the campground reception nor with the police. Rumours fly in a campground; you risk being stuck with the nickname Mr TP for the rest of your stay.
2. Go buy a pack of toilet paper and a can of the cheapest toilet deodorizer you can find in the camp supermarket, named "Tender Petals" or similar.
3. Wait till your neighbour goes to the beach, and then empty the entire can of deodorizer in his tent or camping car, on the mattresses and his clothes. When you finish, proceed to mummifying his tent and his car, if possible also his dog, with the rolls of toilet paper.
4. Find a permanent marker pen and write in big letters all over his car: "I am a stinking toilet paper thief!"
5. Don't forget to take the toilet paper he stole from you.

Expert Opinion

I recently read an article in a camping magazine about a campground manager who stole over 7,300 rolls of toilet paper from the campers in one season. He then sold them in the campground supermarket at high prices.

Testimonial

During a campground social event I took the microphone and told everyone that my neighbour, Mr Martin, had stolen my toilet paper. Everybody booed him and he had to leave the campground that night, after having to pack up his tent in the rain.
Gina, 39, banker, London

THE ZIP OF YOUR TENT IS STUCK

The situation:

You are in your tent when suddenly you really have to go. But there is a problem: the zip of your tent is stuck. No matter what you try you can't open it; you will not be able to come out in time.

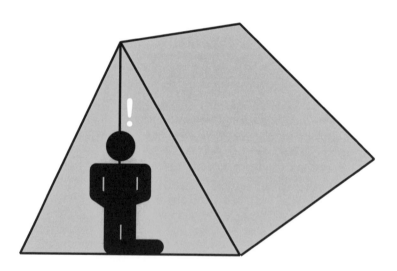

SOLUTION: The Magic Box

1. Take your flask, remove the cap and place it on the floor.
2. Crouch over the flask. Press on both sides of the tent in order not to fall.
3. Do your deed aiming with precision the bottle neck.
4. When done, sacrifice five pages of your holiday reading to wipe off.
5. Close the flask as quickly as possible, or it will smell as if you farted ten times in under a minute.
6. Get dressed. Call for help, and as soon as you are out, throw your flask away. Here's hoping that some other camper won't pick it up thinking they made a great camping gear find.

Expert Opinion

If this happens during the night, do the same thing, but make sure never to turn on a light in your tent. It would create a shadow puppet theatre for other campers to enjoy.

Testimonial

Unfortunately I did not know this technique. I yelled: "Ouhhh heeelp-eh, I'm stuuuck in the teeeeent!" and "Hurry up, I have to go to the loo!" Two minutes later a neighbour came to my rescue, tearing through my tent with a knife. He found me doing it into my sleeping bag…
Damien, 34, insurance assessor, Tring

THE TOILET IS DISGUSTING, AND YOU ARE BAREFOOT

The situation:

You are enjoying the relaxed holiday dress code and spend most of your holiday barefoot. Most of the time this doesn't lead to any problems, except in this case: you arrive at the toilet only to find out that the toilet floor is disgustingly dirty.

SOLUTION: Indoor Athletics

1. Estimate the exact distance separating the door of the stall from the toilet seat.
2. Take three steps backwards.
3. Run then use the momentum to jump with your feet together in order to land on top of the toilet seat, with one foot on either side.
4. Balance yourself and lower your pants (if of course you're wearing them in your holiday free spirit).
5. Do your deed.
6. Jump out of the toilet.

Expert Opinion

The sportier types will even attempt the same method with a Fosbury Flop that will make them land sitting down.

Testimonial

Usually in such situations, I will go find a high-pressure water cleaner. Seeing as I didn't have one handy I tried to follow your method. I landed with my both feet inside the toilet.
Yann, 42, telecoms, Kettering

THE TOILET PAPER IS RIDICULOUSLY EXPENSIVE

The situation:

The minimart in your campground sells toilet paper at three times the normal price. It's scandalous! There is no way you will compromise your holiday budget because of some store manager who wants to make money out of you.

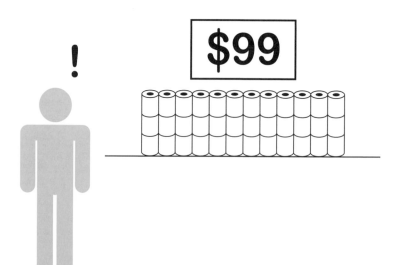

SOLUTION: The Win-Lose

1. Go see other campers to tell them together you could all fight the overpriced toilet paper.
2. There is only one way to win in this battle: you have to unite and buy toilet paper in bulk with other campers.
3. As you are the Chief Toilet Paper Negotiator, you should take the toilet paper orders of all other campers.
4. Go to the supermarket and present yourself as "Head of Camp Toilet Paper Ordering"
5. Tell the manager that you would like to buy 4,000 rolls of paper, but that he should lower the price threefold.
6. If he refuses, go back to the campers and unite them also for a group purchase of toilet brushes and air fresheners. He will have to cede.

Expert Opinion

Seeing as the price of toilet paper continues to rise, I am buying toilet paper in bulk from the factory. I receive a truckload of toilet paper every January.

Testimonial

Five years ago I was on holiday in a village in the South of France. The campground supermarket was selling four rolls for 23 euro (single-layer only too). I organized a demonstration in the neighbouring village. There were 400 of us holding up banners like "Free Toilets For All".
Joe, 38, financial analyst, London

YOU ARE FOLLOWED BY A CLOUD OF POO FLIES

The situation:

You come out of the toilet and a cloud of poo flies starts swirling around you and won't stop following you. It is quite annoying because all other campers will know what you were doing. What's worse, they will see you as a big turd from then on.

SOLUTION: The Fly-Tamer

1. As soon as you see someone you know (even if only in passing), go towards them.
2. Ask them if they've seen Dennis by any chance.
3. Before they manage to respond, continue: "It's because he lent me these shorts and since then these poo flies keep following me around! I don't know what he did with these shorts but I would really like to give them back to him as soon as possible!"
4. Repeat this with any other person that crosses your path and create a wonderful reputation for your friend Dennis.
5. Then, to get rid of the flies, quickly get into your car.
6. Stay in the car until the last fly has tired of waiting for you and gone to find another victim. For your information: this could take up to two hours. Hungry poo flies are very patient.

Expert Opinion

Mind you, some poo flies can smell a fart (even a lighted one) released 2.6 km away. If they can't find something else to eat in their vicinity, you risk being followed by over 1,500 flies.

Testimonial

As I was leaving the toilet, there were around 300 flies swirling around me. I thought it would be a good idea to go back into the toilet and spray myself with the cheap air freshener with a citrus scent that I found in there. But they were still out there, waiting for me. It was only after I wrapped myself entirely in apricot-perfumed toilet paper that I managed to get them off track.
Peter, 35, sales, Hull

THE SUPERMARKET DOES NOT CARRY YOUR FAVOURITE TOILET PAPER

The situation:

Like everyone, you too have your favourite toilet paper brand that you can't do without. You are horrified when you find out that the local supermarket does not carry your preferred toilet paper.

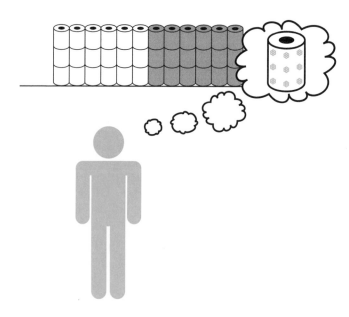

SOLUTION: The Triple-Layered Apricot Solution

1. Don't panic, you will not be forced to not go to the toilet for three weeks. We will find a solution together.
2. Think about what the reasons are you like that toilet paper so much. Is it its quadruple layering? Is it its Wild Violet perfume? Or maybe its floral motif?
3. Make a list and prioritize your criteria. Then go to the supermarket and find the toilet paper that gets as close as possible to your favourite brand.
4. Use this new toilet paper during your entire holiday. A bit of a change will do you good, and you will be able to tell your friends stories about this adventure when you go back.

Expert Opinion

If you recognize yourself in this situation, never go to exotic countries. You are absolutely not ready to wipe your bum with banana leaves.

Testimonial

When I was in New Zealand I found some extraordinary toilet paper. It has six layers, of which three are doused with aloe vera, two are organic cotton and one is silk. It is double perfumed: Japanese Cherry and Spring Pear. I started importing it. Contact me if you would like to order some.
Samantha, 56, importer, Falkirk

THE TOILET IS TOO FAR TO REACH IN TIME

The situation:

You are sleeping profoundly when you are woken by a sudden urge to go to the toilet. You really can't see yourself running 500m to the nearest toilet in your PJs, pocket lamp in hand.

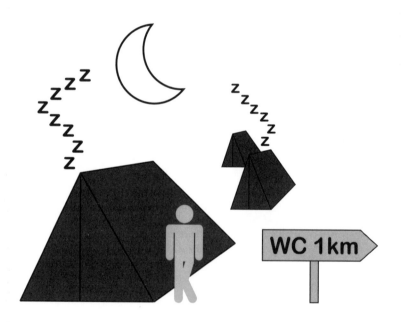

SOLUTION: The Welcome Present

1. Go towards your neighbour's tent.
2. Do your deed in front of his tent.
3. Get up at dawn the following morning.
4. Go to the camp manager and tell him: "My neighbour pooped in front of his tent during the night! Come see, it's disgusting."
5. Ten minutes later, observe your neighbour being evicted from the campground. A piece of advice: look surprised if he looks at you.
6. Take full advantage of your new extra-large plot.

Expert Opinion

I always have an inflatable toilet in my tent.

Testimonial

While I was doing my deed in front of my neighbour's tent I lost my balance and fell on his tent. While trying to get up I heard the zip opening and found myself naked, pants around my ankles, face to face with my neighbour and his pocket lamp.

Michael, 29, sales admin, Brighton

PROBLEMS ENCOUNTERED WHEN ENGAGING IN HOLIDAY ACTIVITIES

During holidays we get the opportunity to discover many new activities. However, many of them can give you a violent urge to go to the toilet.

What should you do when you really need to go during a visit to the zoo? And how can you do it when you are 20 metres under water or 20 metres above ground on a chairlift?

Find out in the following pages how to combine wonderful new adventures with the pleasure of doing your deed!

The Golden Rules

1. Before any activity, try for at least 20 minutes to do your deed.
2. Avoid any activity where a fitted suit is required that cannot be taken off quickly and easily.
3. Avoid any activity that involves being shaken (trampoline, being pulled by a banana float…)
4. Consult the instructor beforehand what his advice is for doing your deed while engaging in the activity (better now than later when it's already too late).
5. At the end of the activity, don't ask for your money back if you missed a part or all of it because of your poo issues.

The situation:

While getting on the longest chair lift at the ski station, you are overtaken by the biggest urge to go to the toilet. Telling your neighbours to close their eyes for a few minutes while you do your deed 30m above ground does not seem appropriate.

SOLUTION: The Ice Rod

1. Do not let out any gas. You will be given the evil eye by your neighbours who have come to appreciate the fresh mountain air.
2. Discreetly stick your belly to the ice cold protection rod. The cold will temporarily block the transit.
3. If the urge is no smaller (or is even bigger), place one of your frozen sticks between your buttocks. Effectiveness guaranteed!
4. Once the chair lift comes to the top, don't think for a second that you are out of the woods. Take off the skis and run towards the nearest restaurant to do your deed. Be careful, once you enter, the thermal shock will reactivate your transit.

Expert Opinion

If you have stunk up the restaurant toilet, put on your ski goggles and hat so that people won't recognize you later.

Testimonial

When the chair lift was coming to the top, I was about to burst. I didn't have time to take the skis off. I skied down the steps leading towards the toilet. I did my deed with skis on. It was the Schuss position.
Leo, 28, accountant, London

AT AN AQUATIC AMUSEMENT PARK, IN THE QUEUE

The situation:

You have been queuing for a good 40 minutes for a ride down a water slide at the water amusement park. It is almost your turn when you are taken by a powerful urge.

SOLUTION: The Giant Flush

1. Hang in there; you will have to hold it until the take off.
2. Loosen your swimsuit cord; it is pressing you in a bad area.
3. Once at take-off, hold on to the handles and squat.
4. Swiftly take off your swimsuit and do your deed in front of the dumbfounded lifeguard.
5. Before he can do anything about it, slide down the water slide as fast as you can, as your deed will follow right behind you. (Our advice: the "Torpedo Penguin" technique is the fastest.)
6. Once you splash-down, leave the pool immediately.
7. Leave the water park as fast as you can.

Expert Opinion

Personally I use the technique I learned while in the Special Forces: I stop mid-slide, lower my swimsuit and do my deed.

Testimonial

I was the only one going down so I had all the time in the world to do my deed. Once I came down, the deed was only seconds behind me. I went and told the lifeguard that the child belonging to the lady in a blue swimsuit had relieved himself in the arrival pool. I also told him just how scandalous I thought such behaviour was.
Dominic, 33, CSR, Sandringham

IN A SQUAT TOILET, WEARING ROLLERBLADES

The situation:

During a spin in your rollerblades you are taken by a strong urge to poo. You go to the nearest public toilet you come across. No luck: it's a squat toilet.

SOLUTION: WC Free Ride

1. Never, ever attempt to do a squatting deed when wearing rollerblades; you are guaranteed to fall.
2. At the entrance, turn around. Slowly! The ground is probably very slippery.
3. Back into the toilet.
4. When in the toilet, wedge your rollerblades between the wall and the ground on each side.
5. Lower your pants and squat.
6. Help balance yourself by holding on to the rope hanging from the flush.
7. Do your deed (keep in mind that due to rollerblades you are taller than usual; it gives you different sensations).

Expert Opinion

According to a study commissioned by an insurance company, 14% of sprained ankles of those under 25 are due to falls in squat toilets whilst wearing rollerblades.

Testimonial

I was successful in my first attempt, and stupidly this gave me confidence. The second time, while doing my deed and attempting to balance myself, I put my hand in the hole...
Terry, 35, freight agent, Carmarthen

YOU ARE SPORT FISHING, AND YOU JUST CAUGHT AN ENORMOUS SWORDFISH

The situation:

You are Sport Fishing, way out in the open sea. You are struggling with an enormous swordfish that you just caught. The struggle is so stimulating that you suddenly feel the need to go to the toilet immediately.

SOLUTION: The Magic Wand

1. Don't lose your hold; you will go to the toilet with fishing rod in hand.
2. Get off your seat and start backing towards the boat toilet, never letting go of your fishing rod.
3. Do your deed with the fishing rod in hand, and try not to struggle too much (it's better to let go a bit more of the line than fight the fish and get thrown against the walls while pooing).
4. Come back out, resume your position and land your prize catch.

Expert Opinion

When will they ever invent a seat for fishermen that serves also as a toilet? It would make it possible to do both struggles at the same time.

Testimonial

The swordfish was so strong that it pulled me out of the toilet and dragged me all the way to the bridge, butt-naked.
Piers, 55, director, East Sheen

YOU ARE SCUBA DIVING

The situation:

You are scuba diving when you feel a strong urge to poo, most likely due to the mounting pressure underwater that is pressing against your stomach. The problem is that you are wearing a tight wetsuit that doesn't allow for normal evacuation.

SOLUTION: The Secret Shell

1. When your buddy (diving is always done in pairs) asks you if everything is ok, try to indicate to him that you need to poo.
   NB: Unfortunately the international diving federation has still not thought of inventing a hand signal to say: "Buddy, I need to poo."
   Try holding your stomach and grimace.
2. When your buddy understands what you are trying to tell him, get him to use his knife and make a slit in your wetsuit in the middle of your bum. Warn him to do it gently: he should only cut your wetsuit and your swimsuit, not your buttocks.
3. Once your wetsuit is slit, do your deed under water. The fish will approach you, curious about the new brown fish in their territory.
4. At the end of the dive, tell your instructor: "I want a refund! I was freezing my bum off during the whole dive because your wetsuits are full of holes!"

Expert Opinion

Be careful; I heard that below 20 meters, you could get an enema that way. Let me just mention that I am currently developing surfing and diving wetsuits that would have a zip at the strategic spot.

Testimonial

I used this technique but when I finished the 'brown fish' followed me everywhere; I could not get rid of them.
Gavin, 43, stock market trader, Ipswich

YOU ARE AT THE ZOO

You are at the zoo and you have eaten too many peanuts intended for the monkeys. Serious error.

ZOO WC

SOLUTION: The Smoke-Out

1. Stop eating those peanuts!
2. Go towards a pen (preferably one with goats or guinea fowls rather than a tiger or elephant pen).
3. Go into the pen.
4. Urinate on a tree. This strong odour will attract all the animals of the pen, curious to see what new mammal came to mark his territory in THEIR pen.
5. While the animals are busy sniffing, go towards their hut.
6. Crawl into the little hut and do your deed.

Expert Opinion

Careful, while you are doing your deed an animal could leave the group and come sniff your bum. If it happens to be the dominant male, he could come charging at you. You can't really blame him; you're essentially shitting in his living room.

Testimonial

I was in such a hurry that I didn't even notice that one wall of the hut was actually a glass wall that allowed the visitors to see the secret life of animals in their habitat. I think that day they got their money's worth.
Ben, 28, designer, Tottenham

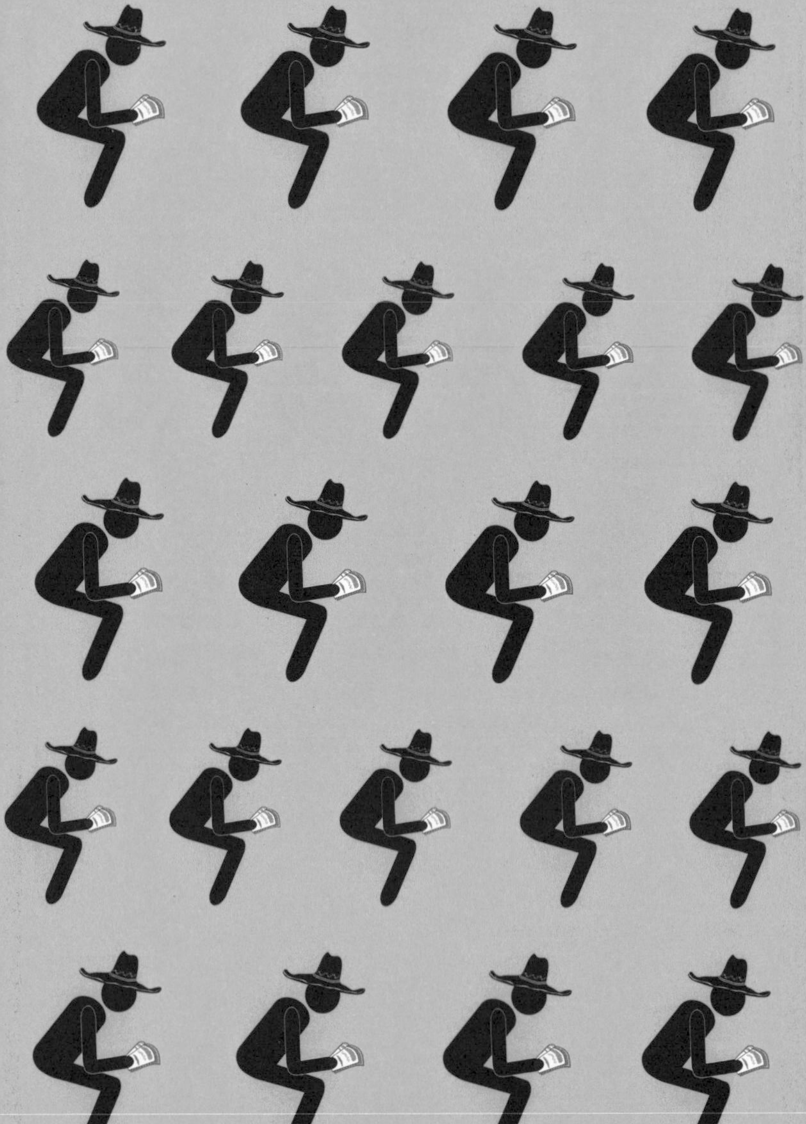

PROBLEMS ON THE WAY
TO YOUR DESTINATION

Means of transport can quickly become a mobile prison. The waiting in a seated position (not unlike the position when sitting on the toilet seat) can become unbearable. Bus, car, plane… they can all make you suffer!

How do you do it when a bus doesn't have a toilet? How do you not get knocked about from one side of a ferry toilet stall to the other when sailing through rough waters?

Find out on the following pages how to reconcile a long journey and an all-encompassing urge to go to the loo.

The Golden Rules

1. Never do your deed on the side of the motorway (you can cause accidents).
2. Take advantage of any opportunity to do your deed normally (one never knows when one will next find a toilet).
3. If you usually need time in the toilet, alert the driver to that fact (so that he doesn't leave without you at the next stop).
4. Never fart (the smell is reinforced in enclosed spaces)
5. Never let go of the steering wheel of your RV thinking that you can quickly go to the toilet.

THE REST STOP TOILET IS DISGUSTING

The situation:

It's the first day of your vacation and you are driving towards your 5* hotel and fantasizing about its magnificent toilets.
But an overwhelming urge takes you and you can't hold on; you have to stop at a service station, only to discover that the toilet is revolting.

SOLUTION: The Road Safety Tips

1. Go to the service station shop without grimacing and wiggling around.
2. Buy a new tyre.
3. Go back to the toilet with your tyre.
4. Place it on the toilet, make yourself comfortable and do your deed.
5. Take the tyre back to the shop and demand to be reimbursed, saying indignantly: "Your tyre smells of poo!"

Expert Opinion

There are better things to use than tyres: steering wheel covers! Place it on the seat before doing your deed. I have an imitation sheep skin cover on my toilet seat at home. It is soft and keeps you warm in the winter.

Testimonial

Instead of the tyre I bought a safety triangle that I placed on the seat. Once I finished, the horrific odour shocked even me and I could barely breathe. I had the good idea of using the triangle to alert others to the presence of toxic gasses in the toilet.
Bob, 33, PR, London

IN A BUS THAT HAS NO TOILET

The situation:

You are in a bus that is taking you towards your holiday destination. You have to go really badly, but the next stop is not for another two hours.

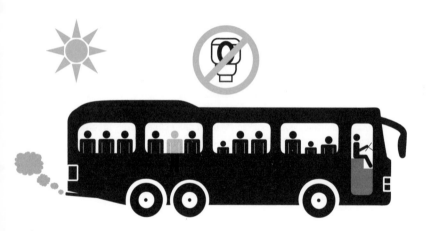

SOLUTION: The Good Deed

1. Go towards the driver, but don't mention your problem explicitly as you may get nicknamed Poomeister by other passengers.
2. Say to him: "We need to stop. Sarah, that cute blonde in the last row, really has to poo. She can't hold it anymore."
3. Go on: "For the past hour she has been holding her stomach and farting. We've all had to move to the front of the bus."
4. Take the microphone and tell everyone: "It's ok Sarah, we will stop at the next rest stop. You will finally be able to relieve yourself. Hold on, we're all with you!"
5. When you reach the rest stop, say you need to stretch your legs so that you can distance yourself from the group and go relieve yourself.

Expert Opinion

There is a new EU directive for buses with toilets: the use of a safety belt is mandatory when sitting on a bus toilet. The European Commission is seriously considering amending the directive to include mandatory use of airbags in the bus toilet.

Testimonial

I went to the driver and asked him as discreetly as possible to make a stop. He took the microphone and announced to the bus: "OK, we will make a two minute stop; Quentin has a brown sausage poking out of the hole."
Quentin, 36, facilitator, Exeter

ON A FERRY GOING THROUGH SOME ROUGH SEAS

The situation:

You are crossing the sea in a ferry. The sea is rough, and the ferry is pitching strongly on the waves. You have to do your deed in a toilet booth that sways by 30° every three seconds.

SOLUTION: The Viking About-Face

1. Don't approach the task as usual: turn towards the toilet and ride it as if you were mounting a motorcycle or a horse. If done correctly, you are now turned towards the water tank.
2. Hug the water tank tightly.
3. Don't lose your grip on the water tank while relieving yourself, to counterbalance the movements of the boat.
4. Don't wipe off as usual. If you let go of the water tank, you risk being thrown towards the walls of the stall. Instead, lay flat on the ground while wiping (better a dirty t-shirt than a dirty bum).
5. Come out of the toilet feeling justly proud that you did your deed like a true seaman.

Expert Opinion

When I think about those cruises for the elderly, I often wonder how tough it must be for them when they go to the toilet in rough seas.

Testimonial

When I was in the about-face position, the door of the stall opened. The people waiting outside thus saw me in this unusual position. They must have thought that I really liked that toilet.
Mark, 43, architect, Derby

IT'S TOO LATE

The situation:

You are taking a trip in a minibus and you start feeling a very strong urge to go to the toilet. Knowing that there is no way you can hold it until the next scheduled stop in two hours, you ask the driver if he could please stop. Being already behind schedule, he refuses. 30 minutes later, the drama begins.

SOLUTION: The Kekomi

We won't lie to you; you are in deep… trouble. The following will require much courage and your self-esteem is likely to suffer a blow.

1. Try eliminating the smell somewhat by opening all windows, even if it's only 2°C outside.
2. Go towards the driver as normally as possible. Don't grimace.
3. Tell him: "You should have stopped when I asked you, you asshole! I've crapped my pants now!"
4. Tell him to stop immediately and open the baggage compartment so you can find some clean clothes.
5. Clean off with water from the bottles intended for the group.
6. Put on clean clothes and get back on as if nothing happened.

Expert Opinion

The smell that a bus seat absorbs in such a situation takes over a month to disappear. This will be your vengeance for your tormenter driver.

Testimonial

Even after all that, the bloody driver still wouldn't stop!
Mick, 30, IT support, Staines

IN AN RV

You are in an RV equipped with a toilet. You have to do your deed in the tiny toilet it offers.

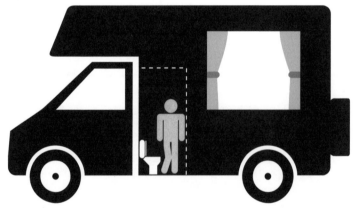

SOLUTION: The Space Shuttle Technique

Important: *Don't forget to open the ventilation hatch. Considering the small size of the space you will otherwise suffocate in less than four minutes.*

1. Once seated, don't bend forward while pushing; the toilet is so tiny that you risk hurting your forehead on the water pipe.
2. Don't turn your head to the left; you will knock over the tins that you put there because there was no space anywhere else.
3. Don't turn your head to the right because you will hit the toilet paper holder.
4. Try not to fart while doing your deed, as there are people eating less than 50cm from you, and the wall between you is paper thin.
5. Don't come out with your pants around your ankles to ask where the toilet brush is: it's fastened under the toilet seat.
6. Carefully close the toilet seat cover (don't break it; it serves also as the chopping board for the vegetables in your kitchenette).

Expert Opinion

The first RVs had toilets under the driver's seat. The driver simply had to lift the cushion to do his deed. The problem was that it overflowed at each turn.

Testimonial

I weigh 24 stone. I could not get out of the toilet. My family had to call the local firemen who cut the RV around the toilet so that I could come out. It was our best friend's RV...
John, 54, accountant, Rutland

YOU HAVE TO BOARD
THE PLANE IMMEDIATELY

The situation:

You are in the airport toilet. Just as you are about to start relieving yourself, you hear your name being called, asking you to board immediately.

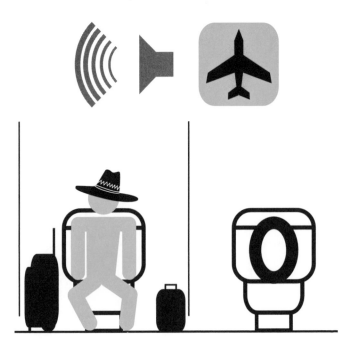

SOLUTION: The Voice From the Distance Technique

1. Tap the door to draw attention.
2. Yell: "Yeees, it's meee, I'm coming! I'm in the toilet! Wait for me!"
3. If someone responds, continue relieving yourself.
4. If not, keep trying: "I'm almost done! I'm just wiping off! I'll be there in two seconds!"
5. Run towards your gate when finished.

Expert Opinion

Don't panic and run out with your trousers around your ankles to tell the airport personnel that you only need two or three minutes more to finish.

Testimonial

In the rush, I wiped my bum with my boarding pass...
George, 36, technician, Cambridge

YOU STUNK UP THE BUS TOILET

The situation:

You do your deed on the bus, and it smells very bad. It's actually impossible to breathe. When you open the door, all the other passengers will give you angry looks.

SOLUTION: The Empire Strikes Back

1. Come out of the booth and looking cross.
2. Go towards whoever was in the toilet before you. If you don't know who that is, just go to a random person, but make sure they are smaller than you.
3. Look them in the eye and yell: "When you are ill like that you don't go to the toilet! I couldn't breathe in there because it stinks so much! I couldn't even do my own deed!"
4. Add: "Do you think you're at home or what?"
5. Go back to your seat.

Expert Opinion

After that you could also take the microphone and say: "Gerry isn't well. Does anyone have any anti-diarrhoea pills?"

Testimonial

I took on a guy who was sleeping. I yelled at him that pretending to sleep wouldn't help him. Everybody thought it was him who stunk up the toilet. Ann, 34, computer programmer, Toronto

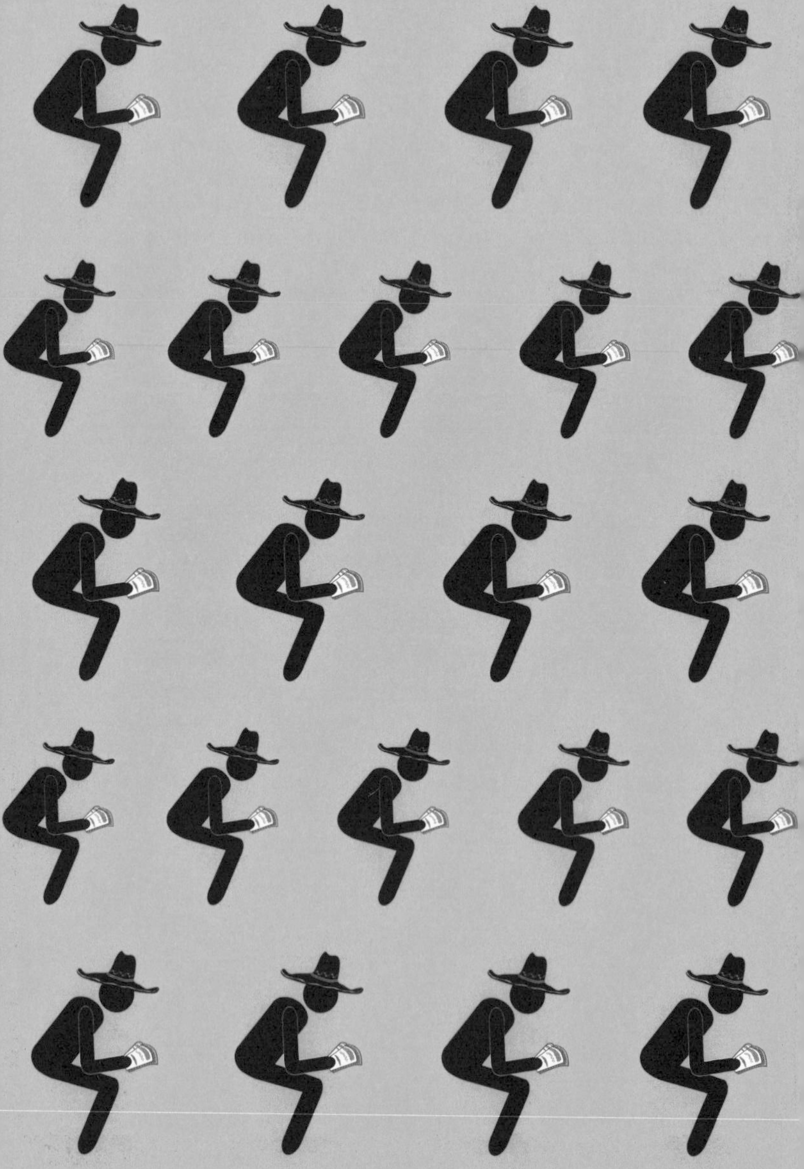

PROBLEMS AT THE BEACH

The beach and the sea are wonderful places, but not necessarily equipped with toilets, and often overly crowded. The problems you can encounter on the beach or in the sea can quickly become quite dramatic. Without some imagination you will not be able to find any solution for your big problem.

How to do your deed without suffering after you've sunburnt your buttocks? How to do it when you are on a surfboard in the middle of the sea? How to do it when the beach is really crowded and doesn't have enough toilets to accommodate everyone?

In the following pages find out the solutions to common problems that can positively ruin your holiday by the sea.

The Golden Rules

1. Always do your deed far enough from the beach (you don't want the smell to engulf the whole beach).
2. Never go to the toilet completely wet (you risk slipping on the tiles).
3. Don't do your deed in the sand (you are not a dog!)
4. If at all possible, avoid plastic toilet stalls (they tend to melt in the hot sun).
5. Don't do your deed in the water (it floats in sea water!)

The situation:

You are on your surfboard in the water when suddenly a violent urge overtakes you. It looks like you have underestimated the well-known laxative powers of sea water.

SOLUTION: The Refreshing Sea

1. Paddle towards the open sea to distance yourself from the rest of the group waiting for the surf. Considering what you have to do, paddle far.
2. Once far enough, climb on your surfboard, feet pointed to the front.
3. Pull down your swim shorts, squat and try to stabilize yourself.
4. Do your deed on the board. Be careful that the waves don't knock you over while you are labouring away.
5. Once finished, face the board toward the waves to let them clean it (aren't waves the most commonly used metaphor for cleanliness in toilet cleaning products?)

Expert Opinion

50 New Tricks to Poo on a Surfboard is the title of the upcoming special issue of *Surf Magazine*. Kelli Sleighter and I have agreed to reveal all our tricks in picture tutorials. You will also learn that out of ten surfers sitting on a surfboard and waiting for the surf, two are doing their deed.

Testimonial

It has to be said: the position on top of a surfboard, with legs straddled around the surf and buttocks wide apart, is the kind of position that just has to make you want to… Personally, after three waves I usually have to get out of the water as fast as I can.
Russell, 63, masseur, Southampton

IN A MOBILE TOILET ON THE BEACH

The situation:

You are at the beach when you suddenly really have to go.
There is only a plastic mobile toilet and you will have to use it.
It's at least 40°C inside and it reeks.

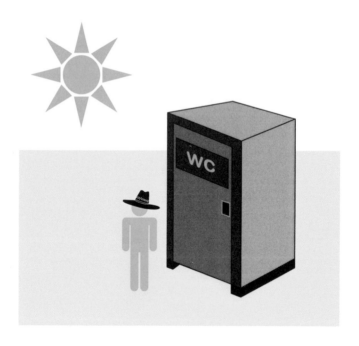

SOLUTION: The Survival Kit

1. Go to the beach boutique to buy goggles, a snorkel and a buoy.
2. Before going into the stall, blow up the buoy and put on the goggles and the snorkel.
3. Put the buoy on the seat and sit on it.
4. Once seated, slide the snorkel through the cracked door so that you can breathe clean air from the outside.
5. Do your deed in this position.
6. Wipe off, continuing to breathe through your snorkel.
7. Come out and give the buoy to the first kid that crosses your path.

Expert Opinion

Careful: if the temperature rises above 45°C, the plastic of the mobile toilet will get soft and you run a risk of finding yourself several feet lower, in a bad position inside the toilet bowl.

Testimonial

I was sick and stayed in the toilet for over an hour. During this time, the high tide came and took the cabin (it was an exceptionally high tide). I ended up floating in the sea for a while inside the toilet stall before getting airlifted to safety by a sea rescue helicopter. And the next day I was of course the cover story of all the local newspapers.
Jim, 43, record executive, Vancouver

THERE'S ONLY ONE TOILET AT THE BEACH, WITH 30 PEOPLE IN THE QUEUE

The situation:

You are at the beach and you have an increasing urge to go to the toilet. You are happy to see a public toilet not far from you. But there is a problem: around 30 people are already waiting for their turn.

SOLUTION: The Cheating Crab

1. Approach the toilet discreetly, by using the crab walking technique. Meaning: walk sideways, and only advance one metre every five seconds, without ever looking at the toilet. The objective: look disinterested.
2. Once you are close enough to the toilet, wait for whoever is in it to come out, and then charge ahead and throw yourself inside.
3. If someone angrily tries to open the toilet door, smash the door in his face.
4. Do your deed, even though the people outside are cursing you.
5. Before coming out, arm yourself with the toilet brush and air freshener.
6. Go out quickly, and defend yourself from the angry mob outside by spraying the air freshener in their faces and beating them with the toilet brush.

Expert Opinion

I always cut the queue because I can't stand having to wait. I have learned to fashion a nunchaku with the toilet brush and the air freshener spray can: I simply tie them together with braided toilet paper.

Testimonial

I am way too polite to do that. I waited for five hours with crossed legs, biting my wallet to hold it in. It's my worst ever holiday memory.
Roland, 42, publisher, London

THE LIFEGUARD SAW YOU DO YOUR DEED

The situation:

You did your deed in the sea without noticing that a lifeguard was observing you the whole time with his binoculars. He is motioning to you to come see him. You fear being fined for polluting the sea.

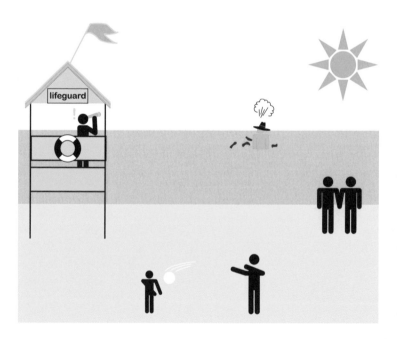

SOLUTION: The Red Flag

1. Go towards him with confidence.
2. Tell him: "So, Mitch Buchanan. Are we a lifeguard or a scatophile?"
3. The lifeguard will look at you funny.
4. Scream loudly, so that everyone can hear you: "You're using your binoculars to ogle holiday makers while they're pooing? Are you enjoying yourself?"
5. Now that everyone is looking, leave the scene while promising the lifeguard you will report him to his superiors.

Expert Opinion

The best position for doing your deed in the water is floating on your back, in the (chocolate) starfish position.

Testimonial

The lifeguard screamed at me through his megaphone: "You, in the blue swimsuit, shitting in the water there! You have three seconds to get out of the water!" Needless to say the whole beach had their eyes on me.
Steven, 31, lab technician, Leamington Spa

YOU ARE IN THE LUXURIOUS TOILET OF A YACHT

The situation:

A billionaire has invited you to his luxurious yacht for a party. Your host has fed you well and you now have to go to the toilet. You will have to figure out the toilet that is worth about 3,000 times more than your own toilet at home.

SOLUTION: The Louis Vuitton

1. Open the door made of precious wood and go towards the seat made of Murano glass.
2. Put on one of the velvet gloves that you see in the little basket next to the toilet.
3. Carefully lift the toilet cover and sit down on the heated toilet seat.
4. Enjoy this moment, and revel in the fact that you are shitting in such an elegant environment.
5. Press on the emerald stone encrusted in the wall to activate the flush, filled with 250 litres of champagne.
6. Clean up with the toilet brush with a mahogany handle and the hair from a lion's mane.
7. Before going out, spray the place with the bottle of Chanel n°5.

Expert Opinion

Do you know that *Yacht WC Magazine* exists? Every month it shows off the most beautiful yacht toilets from around the world. At the beginning of each month I wait impatiently for its arrival in my mailbox.

Testimonial

Someone warned me that the owner of the boat was a bit weird. I got my confirmation when I went to the toilet: there was a camera above the toilet and I could watch myself doing the deed on a giant screen in the door.
Karl, 36, consultant, Wolverhampton

YOU SUNBURNT YOUR BUTTOCKS

The situation:

You fell asleep on the beach, wearing only Speedos. The next day you wake up with painful sunburn on your buttocks. This will create serious problems when you have to go to the toilet: sitting down will be torture.

SOLUTION: The Polar Circle Technique

1. As soon as you notice the sunburn, unscrew the toilet seat.
2. Put it in the freezer on top of the frozen pizzas.
3. If anyone asks why there is a toilet seat in the freezer, look surprised and say it wasn't you who put it there.
4. At the time of need, take out the toilet seat and put it back on the toilet.
5. Sit down on the cold seat. Seeing as the seat was at -18°C, you won't feel the sunburn anymore.
6. Do your deed.
7. Take off the seat and put it back in the freezer – for next time.

Expert Opinion

When I have this problem I do my deed like a gymnast, hovering above the seat with hands on the side of the toilet, legs straight up in the air and my feet on the door knob. This position has also given me an idea for a book: *How to get fit without equipment in less than five minutes a day, using only your toilet.*

Testimonial

I am a redhead with white skin. My bum is burned all summer, every summer. I developed my own technique: I place cucumber slices and pieces of chicken breast on the toilet seat. It has a very refreshing and relaxing effect. It's good for the skin and besides, it makes a great salad for after!
Darren, 31, payroll clerk, Newcastle

TYPICAL PROBLEMS DURING HOLIDAYS

No matter your destination, there are several problems that you will most likely encounter. They can completely ruin your holidays.

What to do when you are so out of your element that you can't do your deed? How to fish out your sunglasses when they fall in the toilet? How do you minimize your holiday toilet budget?

Find in the next pages the solutions to all the problems linked with the use of toilets on holidays, and really get away from it all!

The Golden Rules

1. Never pay for toilet paper that is twice the normal price just because it is being sold in a tourist town. Negotiate!
2. Never try to hold it in for your entire vacation (this is never the solution).
3. Always remember that alcohol is a potent laxative.
4. Mark carefully which medicine in your holiday medicine supply is for headaches and which one is the strong laxative.
5. Never try to negotiate the price of toilet entrance fee with the person taking care of the toilet.

YOU CAN'T DO IT

The situation:

It's been several days since your holiday began. The new toilet is unsettling you; everything is different. Result: you can't do it.

SOLUTION: The Dump Diet

1. You will have to do everything it takes to relieve yourself of this weighty burden.
2. Drink four litres of coconut milk as soon as you get up.
3. Have a big cabbage salad for lunch.
4. Have four melons for dessert (not the meat, just the skin!)
5. Stay close to the toilet for the rest of the day, because the combination of what you ingested is explosive.
6. If at 4pm you still haven't had to go, order 12 scoops of ice cream. Success guaranteed!

Expert Opinion

I recommend you recreate your home environment as much as possible.
I never leave on holiday without my preferred air freshener (Caribbean Queen), my transparent toilet seat with fishes and shells in it, my lavender-perfumed four-layer toilet paper and my favourite gossip or car magazine that I have read and reread hundreds of times.

Testimonial

At the end of my holiday I finally understood why I couldn't do it. I would always get up around 11 am, while at home I always do my deed at 9:32 am, five minutes after my first coffee at work.
Céline, 33, interpreter, Tring

YOU ARE STUCK IN THE TOILET

The situation:

You go do your deed in a toilet that is isolated and far from people. The problem: the door gets stuck and you can't get out.

SOLUTION: The Toy Library

1. You will have to wait for a toilet cleaner to save you, and it can take 12 or 24 hours. You should therefore find ways to help pass time.
2. Start with a hair spa treatment. Spray your hair with the air freshener. Follow up by rinsing your hair in the water tank by tilting your head backwards, just like when you go to the hairstylist.
3. Then play squash. Fashion a ball out of toilet paper and use the toilet brush as a racket.
4. Do a ventriloquist show for yourself: the toilet seat will be your puppet. Talk with your mouth closed and play with the toilet seat as if it was a talking mouth.

Expert Opinion

This happened to someone I know. Somebody put a 'Do Not Disturb' sign on his hotel room. He was only saved five days later when the hotel manager noticed that the room still hadn't been paid for.

Testimonial

I spent the night in there. I slept on the toilet seat, leaning on the water tank, with a roll of toilet paper as a pillow. I didn't sleep very well.
Julian, 32, file clerk, Andover

YOU DON'T HAVE ENOUGH MONEY TO PAY FOR THE TOILET

The situation:

You arrive at a public toilet with the intention of doing your deed. There is a cleaning lady guarding the toilet. As you are about to leave, you realize that you don't have enough money to pay her.

SOLUTION: The Secret Agent Technique

1. Call for help. Say: "Help! The door is stuck!"
2. As the cleaning lady approaches, keep talking so she can follow your voice to the right door.
3. When she arrives, kick the door violently. Your objective: incapacitate the enemy.
4. Now that the enemy is on the ground, you are out of danger. Run out, and never come back to this toilet.

Expert Opinion

I went to the toilet in one of New York's high rises. It cost $100, but it was the ultimate experience: golden toilet, paper fashioned from hand-beaten aluminium, a 140m² stall, noise reduction, 64 types of deodorant, real fox fur toilet brush, mineral water flush, and two 'wipe-off' attendants!

Testimonial

I went to a low-cost public toilet. A big sign outside said 'Entrance fee: €0.01. I thought I had made a great deal but once inside I discovered everything else was a supplement: toilet paper – €2, toilet seat €1, toilet brush – €1, door – €1.50, light – €0.50, soap – €0.50 and of course the flush – €2 ! All together it cost me over €13!
Hal, 44, court reporter, Blackpool

THERE'S NOWHERE TO HIDE

The situation:

You have been trekking through a bare desert for several days. No brush or shrub on the horizon; nothing. Everything is completely flat. There's nowhere to hide to be able to do your deed without your group being able to see you.

SOLUTION: The Little Curtain

1. Admit to the group that you have to do your deed.
2. This will surely come as a relief to others who no doubt have the same problem (do you really think they're all limping because of muscle cramps from too much walking?).
3. Distance yourself from the group by about 100m.
4. Place your rucksack on the ground. It will serve as a little courtesy curtain.
5. While the group is waiting for you and pretending they aren't watching, do your deed hidden behind your rucksack.
6. While you're at it, reassure everyone watching you from the corners of their eyes that all is well by giving them a thumbs-up and yelling: "It's ok!"
7. Return to the group when finished.

Expert Opinion

Be careful, in a salt desert the sound travels without losing its intensity. A simple fart, even a discreet one, can be heard for over 900m.

Testimonial

When I came back, all other people were scattered about as well, doing their deeds. All you could see were backpacks and heads.
James, 32, technician, Tunbridge Wells

YOU DRANK TOO MUCH
AND YOU ARE DRUNK

The situation:

You're on holiday and you let your hair down with the help of some alcohol. Looks like you overdid it because you are completely drunk. This gives you the urge to go, and you have to do something about it.

SOLUTION: The Drunken Bat Technique

1. Once you spot the toilet, start walking straight towards it.
2. Grab the door handle to enter (several tries may be necessary).
3. Take off your trousers and your underwear.
4. Once you are sitting down, check again that you really did take off your trousers… and your underwear!
5. While doing your deed, counterbalance the spinning toilet by pushing with your hands against the walls (the toilet isn't really spinning, you're just drunk).
6. Don't bend forward to push harder; you will fall and land heavily on the ground.
7. Before coming out, check to see if you put all your clothes back on and that you aren't coming out with the toilet paper roll and/or the toilet brush.

Expert Opinion

The main problem with alcohol is that people can't even find the toilet in time.

Testimonial

I was visiting some friends, French winemakers. The toilets seemed weird; low and cold, but I still went and did it. I was informed the next day that I did it in their bidet. They were so disgusted that they redecorated the entire bathroom. Simon, 41, paralegal, London

YOU CAN'T STOP FARTING

The situation:

You overdid it with the local speciality based on beans, cabbage and coconut. You are farting in scandalous sequence, a fart every two minutes. You risk your friends calling you Fartman for the next three years.

SOLUTION: The Warm Wind Technique

1. Listen patiently your friend complaining about your farting.
2. Explain to him: "It's not me; it's my phone!"
3. Your friend will look at you suspiciously.
4. Tell him: "I bought this app called 'Real Fart 3000' for my new phone. When I receive a message, it makes a farting sound. What I didn't know when I downloaded it was that it also comes with the smell…"
5. Add: "It's horrible, I managed to lock the application and I can't uninstall it. And on top of it, I've been getting spam texts every two minutes since yesterday!"

Expert Opinion

Never go into the swimming pool when you suffer from a bout of unstoppable flatulence! Your friends will think that you are in a Jacuzzi. They will promptly join you to enjoy it as well, only to discover that the source of the bubbles is actually you.

Testimonial

When my friend made a remark about my farting, I yelled at him: "I won't listen to advice from someone who goes to the toilet every 20 minutes and has decimated the group's stock of toilet paper in under two days!" This wasn't entirely fair, seeing as he had been constipated since the beginning of the holiday and only went to the toilet once.
Kenneth, 37, client relation service, Weymouth

The situation:

You are about to use an inflatable toilet, which requires some previous knowledge. Here is some advice on how to use this new, very practical and inexpensive toilet that can nevertheless be somewhat dangerous.

SOLUTION: The Chinese Circus Balancing Technique

1. Before you sit down, make sure that the toilet isn't letting air out, because this could mean your butt will descend into the septic reservoir in under two minutes.
2. Sit down carefully: if you plop down too quickly or too heavily, the toilet could explode.
3. If you usually lean back onto the water tank, don't do it: you will fall backwards, together with the toilet.
4. If halfway through you realize that the toilet is letting out air, kneel next to it and blow it back up with your mouth.
   (We don't like to criticize our expert, but we find it slightly odd that the valve is on the inside of the toilet seat.)
5. When you finish, clean the toilet with the inflatable toilet brush.

Expert Opinion

This toilet (that I invented!) works perfectly. Make sure, however, that you are not the person responsible for emptying it at the end of the holiday.

Testimonial

I find inflatable toilets very practical, but I would like to know which idiot pushed the concept too far and replaced the regular toilet paper with bubble wrap. Not only it squeaks; it pops as well!
Tom, 31, salesman, Penzance

YOU HAVE TO USE AN ECO-FRIENDLY TOILET

The situation:

As you don't want to burden the planet, you opt for eco-tourism. After walking several hours to reach your holiday destination, you are faced with an earth-friendly toilet the like of which you have never used before.

SOLUTION: The Sand Castle Technique

1. Enter the toilet stall made of wood that was carried there on a donkey's back.
2. Draw the fair trade organic cotton curtain.
3. Lower yourself on the seat made of rough wood and be careful not to get splinters in your bum. Do your deed as usual, even if the smell of the wood makes you feel as if you were shitting in a sauna.
4. When finished, take a shovelful of sawdust and throw it over the heap of poo in the hole under the seat.
5. Wipe yourself with promotional leaflets that you were asked to bring along (now you know why).
6. Before going out, disinfect the seat with the lemon slices that you will find in a cup next to the toilet.

Expert Opinion

Never throw a cigarette butt into the hole under the toilet. The sawdust will slowly catch fire and you will soon start feeling your bum getting hot. Not to mention the danger of explosion due to the methane coming from the heap of decomposing poo.

Testimonial

Nobody knew how to use it, which made it stink really badly. Everyone went to the toilet with their spray can of air freshener, thereby contributing heavily to the hole in the ozone layer! I'm not sure if the carbon offset of such toilets is really positive.
Oliver, 24, courier, Luton

YOUR SUNGLASSES FELL INTO THE TOILET

The situation:

Out of curiosity you leaned over to inspect the inside of the toilet bowl, but you leaned a bit too far because your sunglasses fell into the toilet. You will now have to extract them manually.

SOLUTION: The Red Crab Technique

1. Get dressed. Know that what follows won't be pleasant. You'd better follow our advice carefully.
2. Stick a piece of toilet paper in each nostril. This will help you tolerate the odour when you have to bend towards the toilet.
3. Wrap your thumb and your index finger with lots of toilet paper to fashion a protected clamp.
4. Before you bend over, hold your nose with your free hand (the paper corks will probably not be enough).
5. Locate your sunglasses with surgical precision and grab them with your paper clamp.
6. Don't put them back on immediately. Go out and wash them for about 30 minutes with plenty of water and soap.

Expert Opinion

If after rinsing them for a long time they still smell like shit, throw them out. It's helpless.
A little anecdote: a client of mine who is very short-sighted and had corrective sunglasses was once caught by the cleaning lady washing his sunglasses in the next toilet over. He thought he was using a sink.

Testimonial

I was washing my sunglasses for two hours with six different soaps, but they still smelled. Since they were my favourite sunglasses, I kept them. The problem is that every time I put them on, someone inevitably asks: "Did someone step in a dog turd?"
Paul, 56, technician, Whitley Bay

YOU CAN'T FIND YOUR HOTEL TOILET

The situation:

You reserved a room in a huge hotel complex. When you head towards your room to do your deed, you get lost in the many long, empty corridors of your hotel.

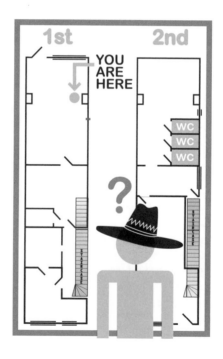

SOLUTION: The Fireman in a Hurry Technique

1. Face the reality: you will not make it to your room in time; especially because the more you need to go, the less capable you are of making sensible decisions.
2. Stop walking, lower your trousers and squat in the middle of the corridor
3. Do your deed on the carpet and wipe off with the curtains.
4. Get dressed.
5. Find the nearest fire extinguisher and spray your deed with it to hide it. Spray some also on the curtains.
6. Go back to the swimming pool.

Expert Opinion

I don't understand why they so often put mirrors in front of the toilet in hotel bathrooms. I can never do it in such toilets.

Testimonial

While I was in the middle of doing my deed, the fire protection sprinklers went off. When I saw the surveillance camera I understood that security were trying to make me stop crapping in the corridor.
Liam, 34, accountant, Wisbech

Q AND A WITH THE EXPERT

Question

I would like to share my experience. I was in a guestroom in Trinidad and their toilets looked a lot like our bathtubs. So I laid down and did my deed in this long toilet. Then I showered and flushed with water from the sink.

Jules, 36, staff writer, Coventry

Answer

Expert: This **was** a bathtub! The toilets in Trinidad are exactly like ours. It's just that your room had a separate toilet.

Q

How do you wipe yourself with a banana leaf?

Pierce, 32, admin, Ipswich

A

It's easy; you do it the same way as with regular toilet paper. Just remember to first remove the bananas.

Q

What would your advice be to someone who would like to begin a collection of toilet brushes?

Frannk, 56, banker, Chingford

A

My first piece of advice would be to set the budget and stick to it. When you begin, never spend more than £50 on a toilet brush — you are a beginner and could be fooled by a counterfeit coming from China. Secondly, invest into a beautiful display shelf or even devote a room in your home to your collection. Thirdly and lastly: don't isolate yourself. Exchange information and advice with other enthusiastic collectors on dedicated forums online.

Q

I once paid £50 for a roll of toilet paper in Uzbekistan. Was I scammed?

Andrew, 29, telecoms, Truro

A

YES!

Q

Can you also use inflatable toilets as a rubber ring that can be dragged behind by a speed boat, like those big inflatable bananas?

Edwin, 32, system analyst, Slough

A

No. Even if the inflatable toilet had handles, I think it would be difficult to do your deed at 50 km/h while being thrown 4m high in the air.

Q

How can one do one's deed in a nudist camp?

Dean, 58, receptionist, Merthyr Tydfil

A

Living in the nude does not mean also doing your deed in front of everyone! Go to the toilet as always, just double check that you don't have some toilet paper stuck to your bum.

Q

I developed a line of air fresheners named "Your Holiday Meal". There are 15 of them, with perfumes such as 'Paella', 'Barbecue', 'Four-Cheese Pizza' and 'Seafood Risotto'. It's not selling much yet. Do you think that the sales will pick up? Any advice?

Matthew, 43, entrepreneur, Basingstoke

A

No, it will never work. My advice: go back to your former employer and beg him to take you back.

Q

In your opinion, which toilet in the world has the best view?

Olivia, 28, consultant, London

A

This is very personal. Anyone can find their own toilet that will please them the most.

Q

What's your worst memory of relieving yourself when on holiday?

Marjorie, 31, marketing assistant, Weymouth

A

In 2005 a wasp stung me in an unfortunate spot while I was doing my deed in an African village. My buttocks tripled in size. The tribe gave me a new name after that: "The White Man with Three Buttocks".

Q AND A WITH THE EXPERT

Q

Can you put a toilet brush in your carry-on when boarding an airplane?
Michel, 33, computer programmer, Coventry

A

No, you can't, because the International Air transport Association (IATA) considers the toilet brush to be a 6th degree weapon. If you cut it in half and tie them together with a small rope or shoe laces you can fashion a mighty nunchaku.

Q

Do you think it's a good idea to mail yourself toilet paper rolls to your holiday destination?
Amy, 28, NGO worker, Cambridge

A

If you are leaving Europe, this is quite necessary. It is also light and therefore relatively inexpensive to mail (USP and DLH have special packaging for toilet paper shipments; contact them). Prepare for the worst (a case of diarrhoea) and envisage 5-6 rolls per day. If at the end of the holiday you have a surplus, you can sell it to a less prepared fellow holiday maker who is suffering with the local material. He will be so happy that he will be willing to pay a lot for the toilet paper and you will earn yourself some extra pocket money.

SURVIVING AN ATTACK IN THE TOILET – SELF DEFENCE

In some more dangerous countries you could be attacked by a thug while you're in the toilet doing your deed. His objective: to steal your money and/or your clothes. No, it doesn't only happen to others. Here is the best technique that will allow you to come out of this attack unharmed.

1. Get up and grab the toilet brush.

2. Hit your aggressor in the face with it.

3. Grab the air freshener can and spray it in his eyes.

4. Put on your trousers and run.

20 OBJECTS THAT CAN ALMOST REPLACE TOILET PAPER

When we are on holiday we don't always have toilet paper available. Fortunately, many objects commonly found on holiday can serve as toilet paper. We selected and tested 20 of them that are commonly used in replacement of toilet paper and asked our expert for his opinion.

1 Bubble wrap
Expert's opinion: Be gentle so that you don't pop the bubbles.

2 A flat fish
Expert's opinion: Don't forget to kill it beforehand. Avoid fish with poisonous dorsal fins.

3 Aluminium Paper
Expert's opinion: Careful, this paper easily tears. Use three layers.

4 A Bedspread
Expert's opinion: My favourite are bed spreads in silk; so soft…

5 A tent
Expert's opinion: Who suggested this one???

6 Bread
Expert's opinion: opt for fresh bread rather than toasted.

7 Cardboard
Expert's opinion: Difficult to handle and painful during use. I would not recommend it.

8 Newspaper
Expert's opinion: The pages with colour photographs can give you a colourful bum.

9 Tree leaves
Expert's opinion: Doesn't work with a spruce tree.

10   A supermarket plastic bag
Expert's opinion: Very practical: it protects the whole hand.

11   A flip-flop
Expert's opinion: even if you intend to wash it afterwards, it's always better to take somebody else's.

12   Socks
Expert's opinion: Be careful because as the saying goes: Socks with holes, hands with moles.

13   A rubber duck
Expert's opinion: Be nice to the duck, don't wipe off with its head.

14   A flipper
Expert's opinion: Careful, they tend to get stuck in the toilets. Good luck trying to explain why one of your flippers is stuck in the sewer pipe.

15   A towel
Expert's opinion: When on the beach, try taking a towel somebody left there. While you're at it, choose your favourite design: a Ferrari, a palm tree…

16   A dishwashing sponge
Expert's opinion: Never use the side intended for scrubbing.

17   A banknote
Expert's opinion: Only use it in countries where a banknote in local currency is worth less than a piece of toilet paper. There are many of them.

18   A map
Expert's opinion: Don't say anything if a few days later your wife has difficulty reading it.

19   An ID card
Expert's opinion: Be nice; clean it before you use it next.

20   A passport
Expert's opinion: Pick an empty page. This could create a new stamp that the customs official will have difficulty deciphering.

There! You finished the book. The time passed quickly, didn't it? Thanks to the erudite advice and sharp opinions of Steven Gooper, your holidays will never again be spoiled by problems encountered in the toilet. You will no longer be disoriented when faced with toilet practices and installations that you have never seen before.

Now that you have the knowledge, the techniques from this book can be a fun topic during your holiday meals. You will see: companions will be captivated by your new knowledge. Keep their curiosity piqued by throwing in phrases such as:

- "Have I told you about the time when I did my deed on a yacht and I was attacked by the owner's lion?"
- "Let me tell you the story of when I chased my neighbour who stole my entire stock of toilet paper round the campground in rollerblades!"

You can go even further: demonstrate the use of toilet brush nunchaku on one of your friends. This will really help create a lively atmosphere!

And since problems aren't only limited to holidays and will follow you to your workplace, pick some other useful books. *How To Poo At Work* and *How to Bonk At Work* will make returning to work after your holiday a complete joy.